Cubesat Engineering

Patrick H. Stakem

(c) December, 2016

Number 1 in the Cubesat series

- Goals for the Book 6
- Introduction 6
- Author 8
- What is a Cubesat? 9
- The Cubesat Design Specification 13
- Mission Design 15
- Space environment 16
- Launch Environment 17
  - Zero G issues 17
  - Vacuum 18
  - Thermal environment 18
  - Orbital Debris 19
  - Electrical Parts selection 19
  - Mechanical and structural Issues 20
  - ESD sensitivity 21
  - Contamination control & materials 21
  - Spacecraft Charging 21
  - Radiation Environment and Effects 22
  - Radiation Hardness Issues for Space Flight Applications 24
    - Cumulative dose and single events 26
    - Mitigation Techniques 28
- Orbit and Ephemeris 29
  - Frames of Reference 30
- Celestial Mechanics 30
  - Orbital Elements, and where to get them 32
  - Ranging 33
  - Orbital Decay 35
  - Disposal 35
- Propulsion 36
- Flight Dynamics 36
- Standards 37
- Cubesat Onboard Computers 42
  - Graphics Processing Unit (GPU) 42
    - Vector Processor 43
  - Memory 45
  - Arduino 45
  - The Raspberry Pi 46
  - PiSat 46

Edison 47
Other Cubesat CPU Options 48
Sensors, Actuators and Mechanisms 49
   Sensors and sensor interfacing 49
   Actuator and Mechanism Interfacing 64
   Spacecraft housekeeping tasks 66
   Power Concerns, and the Cost of Computation 68
Open Source 69
   Features 72
   ITAR 73
Onboard Software 74
NASA's Core Flight Executive, and Core Flight Software 75
Rad-Hard Software 78
   Developing Flight Software 80
OpSys 81
   File Systems 84
   Onboard interfaces 85
Attitude determination and control 87
Electrical Power 88
   Harness 89
   EMI/EMC 89
Thermal Management 89
Telemetry & Command 90
   Cubesat T&C 91
Radio Frequency 92
Ground Segment 93
Structure 94
   Cubesat deployer 94
      P-POD 94
      Other options 95
Safety 95
The Cubesat Operations Control Center 95
   Personnel and roles 99
Mission Planning and scheduling 100
   Anomaly and emergency contingency operations 101
   Off-line analysis & trending; performance assessment 102
   Data Archiving 102
   Spacecraft Simulator 103

Modeling 103
Early on-orbit checkout. 104
Engineering Data Processing 104
Science Data Processing 105
Data Processing Levels 106
Remote Debug, and self-diagnostics 107
NASA System Engineering Process 107
Documentation 107
TRL 109
The T&C handbook 111
Configuration control 111
Faults 111
Engineering Tools 111
Root Cause Analysis 112
FMEA 112
Fault Tolerant Design 114
Redundancy 114
Fault Tree 115
Fault Tolerance 115
Fault Containment 116
Mitigation 116
BIST 116
Integration and Test 117
JTAG support 117
Security 118
Case Studies of Cubesat Missions 120
Brazil's Garatea-L 120
Brazil's Tancredo-1 121
ZACUBE-1 121
NASA Involvement with Cubesats 122
Cubesats on ISS 123
Lunar Cubesats 124
Marco Project 125
Author's picosat 125
Special Cases – Interplanetary Cubesats 126
Constellations 127
Trains 128
Clusters 128

Swarms	129
Case study – Pinesat	130
Complexity	134
Aerospace Failure Case Studies	137
Mars Climate Orbiter	139
Mars Rover Pathfinder	140
Phobos-Grunt	141
Satellite on-orbit collision	143
Wrap-up	143
Cubesat Conferences	144
Organizations offering Cubesat Launch Services	145
Regulators	146
References	147
Resources	153
Glossary	157

Goals for the Book

This book can be used as a reference text for an undergraduate or graduate course, or for an individual wishing to learn about the technology. It is the author's intent that the reader will:

- Understand the Cubesat concept and architecture.
- Understand and be able to address the unique challenges of the space environment.
- Be apply to apply a Systems Engineering approach to the design, implementation, and testing of Cubesat Projects.
- Be able to make engineering trade-offs in system implementation of space flight systems.
- Be able to implement a variety of hardware/software solutions to device interfacing for spacecraft use.
- Be able to remotely debug an aerospace embedded system in a real-time environment.
- Be able to define, implement, and support a Cubesat-based space mission.
- Be able to serve as a member of a Cubesat project Team.
- Pass these skills along to others.

Introduction

This book is an introduction to Cubesats, those popular and relatively inexpensive modular spacecraft that are upending the aerospace world. They have been built and deployed by colleges and Universities around the world, as well as high schools and elementary schools, even individuals. This is because Cubesats are modular, standard, and relatively low cost. The expensive part is the launch, but that is addressed by launch fixtures compatible with essentially every launch vehicle on the planet. Although you may not have much of a choice in the orbit.Cubesats are also flown on high altitude balloons.

At Capitol Technology University, where the author teaches, there is an ongoing Cubesat Project that will receive a free launch from NASA, based on an open competition, scheduled for the end of 2017

Student Cubesat Projects are usually open source, may be world-wide in scope, and collaborative.

At the same time, professionals in aerospace have not failed to consider the Cubesat architecture as an alternative for small-sat missions. This can reduce costs by one or two orders of magnitude. There are Cubesats on the International Space Station, and these can be returned to Earth on a resupply mission.

There is a large "cottage industry' developed around the Cubesat architecture, addressing professional projects with space-rated hardware. NASA itself has developed Cubesat hardware (Pi-Sat) and Software (cfs).

Cubesats are modular, built to a standard, and mostly open-source. The downside is, approximately 50% of Cubesat missions fail. We hope to point out some approaches to improve this.

If you define and implement your own Cubesat mission, or work as a team member on a larger project, this book presents and points to information that will be applicable. Even if you never get your own Cubesat to orbit, you can be a valuable addition to a Cubesat or larger aerospace project. Shortly, two NASA Cubesats will be heading to Mars. The unique Cubesat architecture introduces a new Paradigm for exploring the many elements of our Solar System. Best of luck on your mission.

An upcoming companion volume will discuss Cubesat on-orbit operations, and how to fly your cubesat. I might call it, "The care and feeding of Cubesats."

Author

Mr. Patrick H. Stakem has been fascinated by the space program since the Vanguard launches in 1957. He received a Bachelors degree in Electrical Engineering from Carnegie-Mellon University, and Masters Degrees in Physics and Compute Science from the Johns Hopkins University. At Carnegie, he worked with a group of undergraduate students to re-assemble and operate a surplus missile guidance computer, which was later donated to the Smithsonian. He was brought up in the mainframe era, and was taught to never trust a computer you could lift.

He began his career in Aerospace with Fairchild Industries on the ATS-6 (Applications Technology Satellite-6) program, a communication satellite that developed much of the technology for the TDRSS (Tracking and Data Relay Satellite System). He followed the ATS-6 Program through its operational phase, and worked on other projects at NASA's Goddard Space Flight Center including the Hubble Space Telescope, the International Ultraviolet Explorer (IUE), the Solar Maximum Mission (SMM), some of the Landsat missions, and Shuttle. He was posted to NASA's Jet Propulsion Laboratory for MARS-Jupiter-Saturn (MJS-77), which later became the *Voyager* mission, and is still operating and returning data from outside the solar system at this writing. He initiated and lead the Flight Linux Project for NASA's Earth Sciences Technology Office.

Mr. Stakem is affiliated with the Whiting School of Engineering of the Johns Hopkins University, and Capitol Technology University. Mr. Stakem supported the Summer Engineering Bootcamp Projects at Goddard Space Fight Center for 2 years. He developed and presented Cubesat courses.

What is a Cubesat?

A Cubesat is a small, affordable satellite that can be developed and launched by college, high schools, and even individuals. The specifications were developed by Academia in 1999. The basic structure is a 10 centimeter cube, (volume of 1 liter) weighing less than 1.33 kilograms. This allows multiples of these standardized packages to be launched as secondary payloads on other missions. A Cubesat dispenser has been developed, the Poly-PicoSat Orbital Deployer, P-POD, that holds multiple Cubesats and dispenses them on orbit. They can also be launched from the Space Station, via a custom airlock. ESA, the United States, and Russia provide launch services. The Cubesat origin lies with Prof. Twiggs of Stanford University and was proposed as a vehicle to support hands-on university-level space education and opportunities for low-cost space access. This was at a presentation at the University Space Systems Symposium in Hawaii in November of 1999.

Cubesats began as teaching tools, and remain in that role, although their vast numbers in orbit showed they they have become mainstream.

In what has been called the Revolution of smallsats, Cubesats lead the way. They represent paradigm shifts in developing space missions, opening the field from National efforts and large Aerospace contractors, to individuals and schools.

Even if your personal Cubesat project never gets launched or even built, it will bring you valuable experience to participate. This book will introduce and explain the NASA Systems Engineering Process, which leads from a set of goals to a successful space flight. This model has been in use for decades, and has proven itself to have usefulness. It has been refined as problems were uncovered, and still remains a viable approach to space missions, as well as regular engineering applications.

Cubesats can be custom made, but a major industry has evolved to supply components, including space computers. It allows for an off-the-shelf implementation, in addition to the custom build. There is quite a bit of synergy between the Amateur Satellite

(Amsat) folks and Cubesats. NASA supports the Cubesat program, holding design contests providing a free launch to worthy projects. Cubesats are being developed around the world, and several hundred have been launched.

Build costs can be lower than $10,000, with launch costs ranging around $100,000, a most cost-effective price for achieving orbit. The low orbits of the Cubesats insure eventual reentry into the atmosphere, so they do not contribute to the orbital debris problem.

Central to the Cubesat concept is the standardization of the interface between the launch vehicle and the spacecraft, which allows developers to pool together for launch and so reduce costs and increase opportunities. As a university-led initiative, Cubesat developers have advocated many cost-saving mechanisms, namely:

- A reduction in project management and quality assurance roles .
- Use of student labor with expert oversight to design, build and test key subsystems.
- Reliance on non-space-rated Commercial-Off-The-Shelf (COTS) components .
- Limited or no built-in redundancy (often compensated for by the parallel development of Cubesats) .
- Access to launch opportunities through standardized launch interfaces.
- Use of amateur communication frequency bands and support from amateur ground stations.
- Simplicity in design, architecture and objective .

Multiple cubesatas can be carried as secondary payloads on military and commercial flights, Cubesats, as small, inexpensive units have a higher mission risk tolerance.

Since the initial proposal of the concept, further efforts have been made to define internal and external interfaces made by various developers of Cubesat subsystems, products, and services that have defined the Cubesat 'standard' as it is today. A core strength of the Cubesat is its recognition of the need for flexibility in the definition of standards, and since conception the standard has evolved to ensure that these design rules are as open as possible. The most significant of these further advances in definition have been for the POD systems (in order to meet launch requirements) and the modularization of the internal electronics.

The in-orbit success rate of university-led Cubesat projects (not withstanding launch failures) is around 50%; this is an understandable result of using the Cubesat as an education tool, where development itself is a learning process and in-orbit failure is a disappointment but should not be considered the primary focus. For projects involving significant participation of companies with experience in satellite development, all but one were a success and demonstrated the strength of the Cubesat for non-educational applications. A large number of Cubesat missions have demonstrated significant success in-orbit operations for a sustained period. All Cubesats missions have had technological objectives to some degree, be it the demonstration of devices and system architectures developed in-house, or demonstration of Non-Space-Rated (NSR) Commercial-Off-The-Shelf (COTS) component performance.

A simple Cubesat flight controller can be developed from a standard embedded computing platform such as the Arduino. The lack of radiation hardness can be balanced by the short on-orbit lifetime. The main drivers for a Cubesat flight computer are small size, small power consumption, wide functionality, and flexibility. In addition, a wide temperature range is desirable. The architecture should support a real time operating system, but, in the simplest case, a simple loop program with interrupt support can work.

Earth imaging is a common objective for a Cubesat mission, typically achieved using a CMOS camera without any complex lens systems. As it is a critical impediment to the development of a highly capable platform for mission operations, the testing and evaluation of novel approaches for increasing downlink data rate and reliability is also a common objective. While less common than Earth imaging, real science objectives are becoming increasingly popular as recognition (primarily by NASA) of Cubesat capabilities increase and collaborations between engineering and science groups emerge.

Additional capabilities of proposed future missions either in planning or in development include: space weather monitoring, inflatable de-orbit devices, cosmic ray showers, shape memory alloys, star mapping, data relay, re-programmable computing, nano-meteorid dust, plasma probe, and multi-spectral remote sensing.

Cost reduction in these projects has been achieved through a number of mechanisms, some of which are unavailable to the conventional space industry. The lowest cost yet successful mission is reported to be estimated as under $100,000 (although that mission was not fitted with solar arrays). A typical cost for a university project varies considerably but a very approximate estimation might be from $50,000 to $150,000 for launch and $5-10,000. in parts cost per unit. Piggyback launches have been offered for free to Cubesats by launch vehicle operators and space agencies, negating the majority of launch cost.

Another important and related aspect in the design approach is that of modularity in a complete and integrated Cubesat life cycle, effectively representing a modular system of systems. The accelerated life cycle demonstrated consistently by small satellites, and harnessed by many Cubesat developers, can be further enhanced by the application of modularity to the complete life cycle. Cubesats are ideal teaching tools for aerospace engineering students, even if they are not going to fly.

Cubesats can fly alone, as secondary payloads with other missions such as the MARCO Project to Mars, and in Swarms. The MARCO mission has 2 Cubesat fly-alongs, that separate after launch, and continue to Mars along with the primary payload.

What type of missions do Cubesat's do? Initially, they served as communications relays for Amateur radio. But, they can do essentially what any "big" satellite can do. This includes monitoring space weather, astrophysics, planetary science, or serve as technology demonstrations.

The Cubesat Design Specification

The Cubesat Design Specification, developed by California Polytechnic State University, defines the physical and interface specifications for Cubesats, and gives testing requirements for vibration, thermal-vacuum tests, and shock, as well as safety. Since a Cubesat flys with other Cubesats in a deployment device, and with a primary payload, safety is a concern. Cubesats are expected to have an on-orbit lifetime of less than 30 years.

Here is a synopsis of CubeSat requirements:

Mass

- Each satellite may not exceed 1 kg of mass.

- The CubeSat center of mass must be within 2 cm of the geometric center

Structure

- All edges contacting rails must be rounded. Cubesats must have at least 75% (85.125 mm of a possible 113.5 mm) of flat rail contact with the deployer.

- To prevent cold-welding, raw metal is not allowed as the contact surface of the bottom standoff. Derlin inserts, or a hard anodize are examples of acceptable contact surfaces.

- The outer surfaces of the CubeSats are required to be hard anodized in order to prevent wear between the sliding rails and the CubeSats.

- Separation springs (SSMD-51P recommended) must be included at designated contact points. A custom separation system may be used upon approval by CalPoly/Stanford launch personnel.

- One deployment switch is required (two are recommended) for each CubeSat.

Material

- The use of Aluminum 7075 or 6061-T6 is suggested for the main structure. If other materials are used, the thermal expansion coefficient must be similar to that of Aluminum 7075-T3 (the POD material) and approved by CalPoly/Stanford personnel.

Deployables

- A time delay, on the order of several minutes, must be present between release from the P-POD and any satellite hardware deployment, to allow for satellite separation.

- P-POD rails and walls cannot be used to constrain deployable hardware

Communication

- There must be a time delay, on the order of several minutes to an hour, before all primary transmitters are activated. Low power beacon transmitters may be activated after deployment.

There are emerging standards for larger Cubesats, such as 6U (12 kg, 12 x 24 x 36 cm), 12U (24 kg, 23 x 24 x 36 cm) and 27U (54 kg, 34 x 35 x 36 cm). These allow the cannister to constrain Cubesat deployables such as antennae and solar array. In the original Cubesat specification, this task had to be handled by the Cubesat itself. Even as they get bigger, the standard architecture and modularity of the Cubesat remains a game-changing advantage.

Mission Design

Generally, spacecraft builders think of the complete satellite as having two parts, the bus, and the instrument. The instrument, the science payload, is the reason for the mission. The bus provides services to the instrument, such as structure, data handling, maybe onboard processing, RF transmission and reception, attitude and thermal control, and electrical power. We might also call the bus, the platform. It can be generic, and be used across multiple science payloads. A Cubesat bus can be purchased off-the-shelf, ready to support an instrument and a mission, or can be constructed from the basic components.

Some spacecraft are not on scientific missions, but provide services like the TDRSS satellites, the GPS constellation, and communication satellites such as Dish Network and DirectTV. One of the predecessors to Cubesats were amateur radio relays in orbit. Cubesats can also fly on engineering and technology demonstration missions, improving the maturity of the hardware and software.

I can tell you about almost everything on your Cubesat, except the payload. That is your idea. You might want to look down on Earth (there are some special arrangements needed for Earth viewing), or you might want to look at the Sun, other planets, or the stars. First, you have to define your mission; your reason to build your Cubesat. That drives what instrument(s) the cubesat needs to carry. That is unique to your chosen mission. The Cubesat bus can be "off-the-shelf" or custom built by you. Here, we want to consider, on one hand, the expense of the proven, off-the-shelf parts, and on the other hand, the amount of design, testing, and previous flights' experience that went into those parts. If you do build your Cubesat on your own, conduct trade studies – build versus buy, who has had success with what parts, things like that. There is a vast store of knowledge about successful Cubesat missions, and what went wrong with others. Remember, at the moment, about half the missions fail. But, the statistics are getting better.

From your concept of what you want your Cubesat mission to

accomplish, this book can point you in some correct directions to implement the mission. You defined the WHY, I'll show you the HOW. So, have a mission in mind as your proceed along in the book. It will facilitate the learning process. That's true even if you never build the hardware, but particularly if you go on to building Cubesats for a living.

Let's look at some ways that spacecraft have been used, to give you an idea of what can and has been done.

- Determining soil moisture from space.
- Determining plant/crop health
- Counting cars in parking lots, or traffic monitoring on highways.
- Mapping floods, spills, or forest fires.
- Counting animals in a herd or area and tracking migrations.
- Measuring forest extent and changes.
- Measuring snow pack or ice pack size and changes.
- Measuring land use.
- Detecting and mapping plant disease.
- Mapping poverty.
- Mapping wetlands
- Volcano monitoring
- Quantifying Earthquake and other natural disaster damage.

Notice that all of these are "look-down" missions. Cubesats have alos been involved in "look up" astrophysics and heliophysics missions involving gravitational waves and neutrinos. What you can do with a Cubesat mission is limited only by your imagination.

Space environment

Now, we'll discuss the environment in which the Cubesat will operate, assuming it survives launch. It is not going to sit on your bench or desk. It's going to space.

The space environment is hostile and non-forgiving. There is very little gravity, so no convection cooling is possible, leading to potential thermal problems. It is a high radiation environment, being above the shielding provided by the atmosphere. The Cubesat system is power constrained, and, it is hard to debug and repair after launch, as with almost all missions.

There are differing environments by Mission type. For Near-Earth orbiters, there are the radiation problems of the Van Allen belts and the South Atlantic Anomaly, the thermal and vacuum environment, and the issue of atmospheric drag. This drag causes orbital decay, where the spacecraft slowly descends. There is also a drag factor from the residual atmosphere and the solar wind, and the spacecraft's orbit can be affected in other ways. All Cubesat missions are currently near Earth, although NASA is developing specialized Cubesats for planetary exploration.

Launch Environment

Even without a launch vehicle failure, the launch environment represents the worst case in the path to orbit. There is significant shock and vibration, and a large acoustic environment. This only lasts for a few minutes, but is severe. The spacecraft must be tested beyond the expected launch environment, data for which is available from the launch vehicle provider. The Thermal/Vacuum and Vibration/Acoustics tests are usually referred to as "Shake and Bake."

In addition, we need to examine the structure of the Cubesat to ensure that it is properly vented, so the residual internal atmosphere can vent during ascent.

Zero G issues

Zero gravity, actually, free-fall, brings with it problems. There is no convection cooling, as that relies on the different densities of warm and cool air. Any little pieces of conductive material will float around and short out critical circuitry at the worst possible time. And then, there are the strange issues.

The Hughes (Boeing) HS 601 series of communications spacecraft suffered a series of failures in 1992-1995 due to relays. In zero gravity, tin "whiskers" grew within the units, causing them to short. The control processors on six spacecraft were effected, with three mission failures because both primary and backup computers failed. This is now a well known materials issue, with recommendations for the proper solder to be used. In 1998, the on-orbit Galaxy IV satellite's main control computer failed due to tin whiskers.

Vacuum

The Cubesat operates in vacuum. Not a perfect vacuum, but fairly close. This implies a few things. Lubricant disappear. All the materials outgas to some extent. All this material can find its way to condense on optical surfaces.

Thermal environment

In space, things are either too hot or too cold. Cooling is by conduction to an outside surface, and then radiation to cold space. This requires heat-generating electronics to have a conductive path to a radiator. That makes board design and chip packaging complex and expensive. You get about 1 watt per square meter of sunlight in low Earth orbit. This will heat up the spacecraft, or you can convert it to electrical power with solar arrays.

Parts can be damaged by excessive heat, both ambient and self-generated. In a condition known as *thermal runaway*, an uncontrolled positive feedback situation is created, where overheating causes the part to further overheat, and fail faster.

There can be a large thermal gradient of hundreds of degrees across the satellite, where one side faces the sun, and the other side faces cold space.

Orbital Debris

There is a huge amount of debris in Earth orbit, including old booster units, failed satellites (Zombie-sats), broken solar panels, nuts and bolts, a Russian Space Suit. Space is large, but all of this stuff constitutes a hazard to ongoing missions. We are adding to the problem by launching Cubesats in large quantities.

Cubesats need to comply with the National Space Policy requirement for space debris, which says that small satellites in LEO should re-enter the atmosphere within 25 years from launch.

At Capitol Technology University in Laurel, Maryland, they are addressing this problem with a directed Cubesat mission named TrapSat. NASA though well of this idea, and agreed to provide a free launch for the student designed and built project. This mission will capture and image micro debris, to characterize that environment.

Electrical Parts selection

Another issue is substandard parts, manufactured with an eye to low price and increased sales. Some of these are reversed-engineered or pirated parts. They may bear the same markings and internal identification codes as the legitimate part, and are difficult to tell from the genuine article. This becomes a major problem in military and aerospace applications, although commercial systems are also vulnerable. Software is also subject to "knock-off" versions.

Besides a reliability issue, counterfeit parts cause security concerns in critical systems. A major player in the identification of counterfeit parts is the University of Maryland's Center for Advanced Life Cycle Engineering. It has found that a major source of problems is the large volume of "scrap" electronics sent overseas for recycling and disposal. A lot of this junk finds its way to Ebay or other sources for repackaging and sale.

A counterfeit highly complex chip is hard to detect. You could examine the chip die for full compliance with the design specification, but this is expensive. You could check the product ID on the chip, but this can certainly be faked.

A cheap knock-off chip can be marked properly, and pass functional tests, but fail early due to production issues. Malicious circuitry/code can be included, locked away and hidden from view. Be aware of the problem.

Cubesats tend to use commercial grade products, not their much more expensive cousins, the Space Rated parts. The cost difference can be a factor of 25 or more.

Mechanical and structural Issues

In zero gravity, everything floats, whether you want it to or not. Floating conductive particles, bits of solder or bonding wire, can short out circuitry. This is mitigated by conformal coatings, but the perimeter of the die is usually maintained at ground potential, and cannot be coated due to the manufacturing process.

The challenges of electronics in space are daunting, but much is now understood about the failure mechanisms, and techniques to address them.

Another issue in vacuum is the cold-welding of metallic materials. This occurs when two pieces of material, without an oxide layer, are pressed together. This is facilitated by having very clean surfaces, and a vacuum environment. This affects moving subsystems such as solar arrays and steerable antennas. Early deployment of mechanism is usually not a problem, but mechanisms that have to move throughout the mission can be problematic.

The Cubesat structure has to take into account launch loads, have sufficient stiffnessand be at the same time low mass and inexpensive. There are numerous choices in the marketplace, and a Cubesat structure can be machined to spec. The structure may also need to support deployable mechanisms.

Structural materials must have the same coefficient of thermal expansion as the deployment dispenser to prevent jamming. Specifically allowed materials are four Aluminum alloys: 7075, 6061, 5005, and 5052. Aluminum used on the structure of the Cubesat which contacts the P-POD must be anodized to prevent cold welding in vacuum. Other materials may be used for the structure with a proper waiver.

ESD sensitivity

Solid state devices are particularly susceptible to electrostatic discharge (ESD) effects. These effects can involve very large voltages that cause device breakdown. Certain semiconductor lattice structures that have been damaged can actually "heal" over time, a process called annealing. Passive parts are sensitive to ESD as well. As parts are made smaller, the susceptibility to ESD effects increases. Proper grounding helps with ESD, providing a consistent voltage across components, without significant differences.

ESD can cause parametric changes, which shift the device out of its nominal tolerance region. Over time, parametric changes may go unnoticed as they build, and lead to sudden catastrophic failure.

Contamination control & materials

Proper choice of correct materials for space is critical. Most materials out-gas in the vacuum of space. Lubricants will evaporate, leading to cold welding of mechanisms. In test of the flight article, we would like to hold the cleanliness to class 5-10,000. Materials, components, and systems should be stored in antistatic and sealed bags and handled with gloves.

Spacecraft Charging

Another problem with on-orbit spacecraft is that they are not "grounded." This can be a problem when a potential develops across the structure. Ideally, steps were taken to keep every surface linked, electrically. But, the changing phenomena has been the cause of spacecraft system failures. Where does the charge come from? Mostly, the Sun, in the forms of charged particles. This can cause surface charging, and even internal charging. Above about 90 kilometers in altitude, the spacecraft is in a plasma environment At low Earth orbit, there is a low energy but high density of the plasma. The plasma rotates with the Earth's magnetic field. The density is greater at the equator, and less at the magnetic poles. Generally, electrons with energies from 1-100 keV cause surface charging, and those over 100 keV can penetrate and cause internal charging. As modern electronics is very susceptible to electron damage, proper management of charging is needed at the design level.

Just flying along in orbit causes an electric field around the spacecraft, as any conductor traveling through a magnetic field does. If everything is at the same potential, we're good, but if there's a difference in potential, there can be electrostatic discharge. These discharges lead to electronics damage and failure, and can also cause physical damage to surfaces, due to arcing.

Radiation Environment and Effects

There are two radiation problem areas: cumulative dose, and single event. Operating above the Van Allen belts of particles trapped in Earth's magnetic flux lines, spacecraft are exposed to the full fury of the Universe. Earth's magnetic poles do not align with the rotational poles, so the Van Allen belts dip to around 200 kilometers in the South Atlantic, leaving a region called the South Atlantic Anomaly. The magnetic field lines are good at deflecting charged particles, but mostly useless against electromagnetic radiation and uncharged particles such as neutrons. One trip across the Van Allen belts can ruin a spacecraft's electronics. Some spacecraft turn off sensitive electronics for several minutes every ninety minutes – every pass through the low dipping trapped radiation belts in the South Atlantic.

The Earth and other planets are constantly immersed in the solar wind, a flow of hot plasma emitted by the Sun in all directions, a result of the two-million-degree heat of the Sun's outermost layer, the Corona. The solar wind usually reaches Earth with a velocity around 400 km/s, with a density around 5 ions/cm^3. During magnetic storms on the Sun, flows can be several times faster, and stronger. The Sun has an eleven year cycle of maxima. A solar flare is a large explosion in the Sun's atmosphere that can release as much as 6×10^{25} joules of energy in one event, equal to about one sixth of the Sun's total energy output every second. Solar flares are frequently coincident with sun spots. Solar flares, being releases of large amounts of energy, can trigger Coronal Mass Ejections, and accelerate lighter particles like protons to near the speed of light.

Planets with magnetic fields will trap energetic particles arriving from the Sun into orbiting bands. Earth's are called the Van Allen Belts, after their discoverer. The size of the Van Allen Belts shrink and expand in response to the Solar Wind. The wind is made up of particles, electrons up to 10 Million electron volts (MeV), and protons up to 100 Mev – all ionizing doses. One charged particle can knock thousands of secondary electrons loose from the semiconductor lattice, causing noise, spikes, and current surges. Since memory elements are capacitors, they can be damaged or discharged, essentially changing state.

Galactic Cosmic rays are actually heavy ions, not originating in our solar system. The actual origin is unknown. They carry massive amounts of energy, up into the billions (10^9) of electron volts.

Vacuum tube based technology is essentially immune from radiation effects. The Russians designed (but did not complete) a Venus Rover mission using vacuum tube electronics. The Pioneer Venus spacecraft was launched into Venus orbit in 1978, and returned data until 1992. It did not use a computer, but an attitude controller built from discrete components.

Not that just current electronics are vulnerable. The Great Auroral Exhibition of 1859 interacted with the then-extant telegraph lines acting as antennae, such that batteries were not needed for the telegraph apparatus to operate for hours at a time. Some telegraph systems were set on fire, and operators shocked. The whole show is referred to as the Carrington Event, after amateur British Astronomer Richard Carrington.

Around other planets, the closer we get to the Sun, the bigger the impact of solar generated particles, and the less predictable they are. Auroras have been observed on Venus, in spite of the planet not having an observed magnetic field. The impact of the solar particles becomes less of a problem with the outer planets. Auroras have been observed on Mars, and the magnetic filed of Jupiter, Saturn, and some of the moons cause their "Van Allen belts" to trap large numbers of energetic particles, which cause more problems for spacecraft in transit. Both Jupiter and Saturn have magnetic field greater than Earth's. Not all planets have a magnetic field, so not all have charged particle belts.

Radiation Hardness Issues for Space Flight Applications

A complete discussion of the physics of radiation damage to semiconductors is beyond the scope of this document. However, an overview of the subject is presented. The tolerance of semiconductor devices to radiation must be examined in the light of their damage susceptibility. The problems fall into two broad categories, those caused by cumulative dose, and those transient events caused by asynchronous very energetic particles, such as those experienced during a period of intense solar flare activity. The unit of absorbed dose of radiation is the *rad*, representing the absorption of 100 ergs of energy per gram of material. A kilo-rad is one thousand rads. At 10k rad, death in humans is almost instantaneous. One hundred kilo-rad is typical in the vicinity of Jupiter's radiation belts. Ten to twenty kilo-rad is typical for spacecraft in low Earth orbit, but the number depends on how much time the spacecraft spends outside the Van Allen belts, which act as a shield by trapping energetic particles.

Absorbed radiation can cause temporary or permanent changes in the semiconductor material. Usually neutrons, being uncharged, do minimal damage, but energetic protons and electrons cause lattice or ionization damage in the material, and resultant parametric changes. For example, the leakage current can increase, or bit states can change. Certain technologies and manufacturing processes are known to produce devices that are less susceptible to damage than others. More expensive substrate materials such as diamond or sapphire help to make the device more tolerant of radiation, but much more expensive.

Radiation tolerance of 100 kilo-rad is usually more than adequate for low Earth orbit (LEO) missions that spend most of their life below the shielding of the Van Allen belts. For Polar missions, a higher total dose is expected, from 100k to 1 mega-rad per year. For synchronous, equatorial orbits, that are used by many communication satellites, and some weather satellites, the expected dose is several kilo-rad per year. Finally, for planetary missions to Venus, Mars, Jupiter, Saturn, and beyond, requirements that are even more stringent must be met. For one thing, the missions usually are unique, and the cost of failure is high. For missions towards the sun, the higher fluence of solar radiation must be taken into account. The larger outer planets, such as Jupiter and Saturn, have their own large radiation belts around them as well.

Cumulative radiation dose causes a charge trapping in the oxide layers, which manifests as a parametric change in the devices. Total dose effects may be a function of the dose rate, and annealing of the device may occur, especially at elevated temperatures. Annealing refers to the self-healing of radiation induced defects. This can take minutes to months, and is not applicable for lattice damage. The internal memory or registers of the cpu are the most susceptible area of the chip, and are usually deactivated for operations in a radiation environment. The gross indication of radiation damage is the increased power consumption of the device, and one researcher reported a doubling of the power consumption at failure. In addition, failed devices would operate at a lower clock rate, leading to speculation that a key timing parameter was being effected in this case.

Single event upsets (seu's) are the response of the device to direct high energy isotropic flux, such as cosmic rays, or the secondary effects of high energy particles colliding with other matter (such as shielding). Large transient currents may result, causing changes in logic state (bit flips), unforeseen operation, device latch-up, or burnout. The transient currents can be monitored as an indicator of the onset of SEU problems. After SEU, the results on the operation of the processor are unpredictable. Mitigation of problems caused by SEU's involves self-test, memory scrubbing, and forced resets.

The LET (linear energy transfer) is a measure of the incoming particles' delivery of ionizing energy to the device. Latch-up refers to the inadvertent operation of a parasitic SCR (silicon control rectifier), triggered by ionizing radiation. In the area of latch-up, the chip can be made inherently hard due to use of the Epitaxial process for fabrication of the base layer. Even the use of an Epitaxial layer does not guarantee complete freedom from latch-up, however. The next step generally involves a silicon on insulator (SOI) or Silicon on Sapphire (SOS) approach, where the substrate is totally insulated, and latch-ups are not possible. This is an expensive approach,

In some cases, shielding is effective, because even a few millimeters of aluminum can stop electrons and protons. However, with highly energetic or massive particles (such as alpha particles, helium nuclei), shielding can be counter-productive. When the atoms in the shielding are hit by an energetic particle, a cascade of lower energy, lower mass particles results. These can cause as much or more damage than the original source particle.

Cumulative dose and single events

The more radiation that the equipment gets, in low does for a long time, or in high does for a shorter time, the greater the probability of damage. The Total Ionization Dose (TID) accumulates over time, and actually displaces the semiconductor lattice structure. It causes shifts in the threshold voltage device, and noticeable increased current draw. The damage can become permanent. TID isn't the major concern, as devices become smaller, and the oxide gates become thinner, as technology advances. The higher the voltage, though, the more problematic the effect can be. Analog to digital converters can experience conversions shifts.

These events are caused by high energy particles, usually protons, that disrupt and damage the semiconductor lattice. The effects can be upsets (bit changes) or latch-ups (bit stuck). The damage can "heal" itself, but its often permanent. Most of the problems are caused by energetic solar protons, although galactic cosmic rays are also an issue. Solar activity varies, but is now monitored by sentinel spacecraft, and periods of intensive solar radiation and particle flux can be predicted. Although the Sun is only 8 light minutes away from Earth, the energetic particles travel much slower than light, and we have several days warning. During periods of intense solar activity, Coronal Mass Ejection (CME) events can send massive streams of charged particles outward. These hit the Earth's magnetic field and create a bow wave. The Aurora Borealis or Northern Lights are one manifestation of incoming charged particles hitting the upper reaches of the ionosphere.

Cosmic rays, particles and electromagnetic radiation, are omni-directional, and come from extra-solar sources. Most of them, 85%, are protons, with gamma rays and x-rays thrown in the mix. Energy levels range to 10^6 to 10^8 electron volts (eV). These are mostly filtered out by Earth's atmosphere. There is no such mechanism on the Moon, where they reach and interact with the surface material. Solar flux energy's range to several Billion electron volts (Gev).

The effects of radiation on silicon circuits can be mitigated by redundancy, the use of specifically radiation hardened parts, Error Detection and Correction (EDAC) circuitry, and scrubbing techniques. Hardened chips are produced on special insulating substrates such as Sapphire. The technology is called silicon on insulator (SOI).Bipolar technology chips can withstand radiation better than CMOS technology chips, at the cost of greatly increased power consumption. Shielding techniques are also applied. Radiation hardened parts are much more expensive than standard parts.

EDAC can be done with hardware or software, but always carries a cost in time and complexity. A longer word than needed for the data item allows for the inclusion of error detecting and correcting codes. The simplest scheme is a parity bit, which can detect single bit (or an odd number of errors, but can't correct anything. EDAC is applied to memory and I/O, particularly the uplink and downlink.

Single Event Upsets (SEU) are instantaneous events, caused by highly energetic particles such as Cosmic Rays. This causes momentary bit flips, but is generally not cumulative. Some events may require a reset to affect recovery of state.

Mitigation Techniques

The effects of radiation on silicon circuits can be mitigated by redundancy, the use of specifically radiation hardened parts, Error Detection and Correction (EDAC) circuitry, and scrubbing techniques. Hardened chips are produced on special insulating substrates such as Sapphire. Bipolar technology chips can withstand radiation better than CMOS technology chips, at the cost of greatly increased power consumption. Shielding techniques are also applied. In error detection and correction techniques, special encoding of the stored information provides a protection against flipped bits, at the cost of additional bits to store. Redundancy can also be applied at the device or box level, with the popular Triple Modular Redundancy (TMR) technique triplicating everything, and based on the assumption that the probability of a double failure is less than that of a single failure. Watchdog timers are used to reset systems unless they are themselves reset by the software. Of course, the watchdog timer circuitry is also susceptible to failure.

One concept that is easily implemented, and addresses the radiation damage issue, is called Rad Hard software. This is a series of software routines that run in the background on the flight computer, and check for the signs of radiation damage. The biggest indicator is an increase in current draw. The flight cpu must monitor and trend it's current draw, and take critical action such as a reboot if it deems necessary. The Rad Hard software is a variation on self-check routines, but with the ability to take action if needed. We can keep tabs on memory by conducting CRC (cyclic redundancy checks), and one approach to mitigating damage to semiconductor memory is "scrubbing," where we read and write back each memory locations (being careful not to interfere with ongoing operations). This can be done by a background task that is the lowest priority in the system. Watchdog timers are also useful in getting out of a situation such as the Priority Inversion, or just a radiation-induced bit flip. There should be a pre-defined safe mode for the computer as well. Key state data from just before the fault should be telemetered to the control center. Unused portions of memory can be filled with bit patterns that can be monitored for changes. We must be certain that all of the unused interrupt vectors point to a safe area in the code. There is a lot of creative work to be done in this area.

Orbit and Ephemeris

This section serves as an introduction to satellite orbits. Besides knowing where our satellite is with respect to the Earth, we want to know what is within its field of view, how close it is to a command and telemetry station, and whether it is in sunlight or darkness (for thermal and electrical power reasons). This will get a little physics-intense, but, stick with it. Things behave very differently in space, but the same laws of physics still apply.

Basically, there is gravity in space, but the satellites are in free-fall. They appear to be weightless, but their "mass" remains the same as it always did. Your weight depends on your mass, the local gravity field, and how far away you are from the much larger mass (the Earth). In fact, if you travel about the solar system visiting planets and moons, your mass remains the same, but you weight varies with the size of the planet or moon. Mass is an intrinsic feature of matter. Weight is related to the gravitation field we live in. Isaac Newton gave us this insight in the 1700's.

Most missions from U.S. Facilities to LEO launch from the East coast over the Atlantic from Florida or Virginia. To get to Polar orbit, you launch from Vandenburg Air Force Base in California. One special case of the polar orbit is the sun synchronous orbit. This orbit's inclination is such that the satellite passes over any given point of the planet's surface at the same local time. This is useful for imaging applications where consistent lighting is required. Typically, the spacecraft crosses the equator 12 times a day. Technically, the orbit plane precesses one degree per day, eastward, to match the Earth's motion around the Sun. Nice thing is, there is no eclipse of the satellite, so it always has power for the solar arrays.

Frames of Reference

Frames of reference are 3-dimensional Newtonian references, that we can compare our spacecrafts orientation, with regards to. There are many possible frames of reference, some stationary, some moving. For example, we might choose a frame at the center of the Earth, called the geocentric inertial frame. This is stationary with respect to the Earth, and we can calculate the satellite's position with respect to this frame. We can also assume the surface of the Earth rotates and wobbles a bit with respect to this frame. So, if we want to know when the spacecraft can view, say, your home town, we calculate the position of the spacecraft and your town, in this frame of reference. There is also a solar-based frame, situated in the Sun. This is useful for interplanetary mission. The geocentric inertial frame moves with respect to the Sun's inertial frame. If we are in orbit around Mars, we would used a Mars-centered inertial frame. It is a similar case for the other planets. In any frame of reference, we locate the spacecraft in three dimensions, with three coordinates, x, y, z, with respect to the zero-point, or origin of the frame. It is also useful to know the spacecraft's velocity (in three dimensions) with respect to the frame. These measurements are only valid at a specific time. There is also a Galactic frame.

Celestial Mechanics

How do we describe the position and velocity of something in orbit? We start with F=MA (force = mass times acceleration). Force and acceleration will be vector quantities in three dimensions. The mass is an intrinsic property of, in our case, the Cubesat.

Ok, we have three vector quantities. To get from the acceleration to the position, we need second order differential equations. What this means is, we have (3 x 2) six parameters to define the position and velocity of the spacecraft in space. These parameters will be with respect to a frame of reference.

Now, we are indebted to Johannes Kepler for his work on orbits in the 1700's. He was working on the orbits of the planets around the Sun. His pick of the six parameters to describe a body's position in orbit have become known as the "Keplerian" elements. There are lots of different ways to do it, but this one is the most common. Keep in mind, these six elements are only valid at a particular time, called the Epoch.

The six Keplerian elements, as commonly used are called Inclination, Right ascension of the Ascending node, Eccentricity, the Argument of perigee, the Semi-major axis, and the True anomaly at epoch. Given this data, you know the position and velocity of your Cubesat. I'll tell you where to get these data for your cubesat shortly.

This is the solution to the so-called two body problem. Kepler assumed a large mass (the Sun) with much smaller masses (planets) orbiting it. You can also assume a body such as the Earth with small bodies (Cubesats) orbiting it. Kepler's process tell us where our Cubesat is.

The problem with the two body problem is, it doesn't take into account any other significant masses. For example, the effect of the Moon's gravity on the Cubesat orbiting Earth. The moon does pull the oceans toward it, after all, creating the tides. We can adjust for that, with what is called the Method of Perturbations. But, what about the effects of Jupiter? This leads us to the three, four, and multi-body problem. At the moment, these have not yet been solved, in closed form solution. Some are even difficult to model

We're not going any farther in Orbital Mechanics. You can take the multi-Semester course, and there are a lot of good software tools. You might even come up with the solution to the multi-body problem.

You have all you really need to know to track your Cubesat's position in orbit. From that, you will know what it is passing over, on Earth, and where the Sun is. This is important, because Cubesats only transmit to stations over ground, not the oceans, and you'll need the sun to recharge the batteries.

I just want to mention Lagrangian points. This is where it starts to get weird. Here, we have a "restricted" three body problem, with two large bodies (let's say, Earth and Moon) and one small body (the Cubesat). In this model, there are 5 points where the gravity field has a null. What's interesting about this is, if you put something there, it stays there. Sort of. Disturbances from other bodies will cause some deviations. The really strange thing is, you can place a satellite in orbit around these points in space. There's nothing there, but the satellite orbits around, the same as it would do a planet.

Why do I mention this, besides the fact it is weird? Sometimes, we put satellites there for good reasons. For example, when the James Webb Space Telescope gets launched, it will go to the Lagrange point behind the moon. It will be in an orbit such that the moon is between the satellite and the Sun. The Telescope is a thermal one, so that's a good idea. Minor perturbations from the other planets will require the telescope to adjust its orbit now and then with gas thrusters.

A Cubesat at or in orbit around a Lagrange point is quite feasible.

Orbital Elements, and where to get them

You don't need to track your Cubesat. There is Orbital position as a service. NORAD (North American Aerospace Defense Command) in Colorado, tracks EVERYTHING in orbit, including your Cubesat.

Your orbital elements will be posted to on a website for you to access: How do you know they're yours? Well, you registered with NORAD, and got a reference number for your satellite.

Here's the website. **www.celestrak.com/NORAD/elements**

Ranging

So, how does NORAD figure out where everything is? They have a lot of radar stations around the globe. The data is used for orbit determination and updating of the orbital model. If the satellite is compatible with the active system, a ranging code is sent up, and returned by the spacecraft. This gives more accurate data.

NORAD tracks all detectable orbital entities, from large satellites to space junk, zombie-sats, and the larger pieces of debris, bolts, gloves, as well as near-Earth asteroids.

NORAD puts all this up on a website, in a standard format called the "two-line element" (TLE). This contains the Keplerian orbital elements, the set of data describing the orbit of anything around the Earth, for a given point in time (epoch). It is in a legacy format from the 1960's, that still works. It includes two data items of 80 ASCII charters each (a legacy of IBM punch card format).

Here is the format and contents of Line 1 (courtesy, Wikipedia).

Field	Column	Content
1	01-01	Line number
2	03-07	Satellite number
3	08-08	Classification (U = unclassified)
4	10-11	International Desig. (last 2 of launch year)
5	12-14	International Desig. launch # of year
6	15-17	Internat. Desig piece of launch
7	19-20	Epoch year (lat 2 digits)

8	21-32	Epoch day of year and fraction of the day
9	34-43	1st time deriv, of Mean Motion, divid. by 2
10	45-52	2nd time deriv, of Mean Motion, divid. By 6
11	54-61	BSTAR drag term
12	63-63	Number 0
13	65-68	Element set number
14	69-68	Checksum, Modulo 10.

Line 2

Field	Column	Content
1	01-01	Line number
2	03-07	Satellite number
3	09-16	Inclination, deg.
4	18-25	right ascension of ascending node, deg.
5	27-33	Eccentricity
6	35-42	Argument of Perigee, degrees
7	44-51	Mean Anomaly, degrees
8	53-63	Mean motion, revs per day.
9	64-68	rev. number at Epoch
10	69-69	Checksum, Modulo 10.

Need your data? Get an account with spacetrack.org, and get it on line.

You can also use this service:
http://www.celestrak.com/NORAD/elements/

Need to watch out for debris? Go here:
http://satellitedebris.net/Database/

You can find an open source software orbit model for your Cubesat, and feed it the orbital elements from NORAD. Now you know where your Cubesat is.

If the spacecraft needs to know its own position, it can use GPS services. That's because the GPS satellites are above "Low Earth Orbit," where most Cubesats hang out. To use GPS receivers meant for on Earth usage in Space instead, we need to lower frequency range, and remove the built-in ionospheric correction. The Cubesat can then, on its own, predict when it is in view of a telemetry station, when it should take an observation, and when it can charge batteries. This requires us to implement an orbit model in the onboard software. There is example code, particularly in open source.

Orbital Decay

The atmosphere doesn't really stop abruptly at some point above the planet, it just gets thinner. So, there is always some drag involved from solar panels, or antennas. This is small, but it builds up over time. Large mission like the ISS adjust their orbits periodically, by firing boosters to take the assembly back to the correct altitude. Left uncorrected, the satellite will eventually re-enter the denser points of the atmosphere and burn, due to frictional heating. Actually, we plan for that to happen, and older satellites are deliberately de-orbited so they don't interfere with ongoing missions. Now, every spacecraft mission has to have an end-of-life plan. Even Cubesats. There is a product called "terminator tape" for Cubesats, that is deployed at the end of the mission. It creates additional drag, and causes more rapid orbital decay.

Disposal

By requirement, a Cubesat is required to reenter the Earth's atmosphere within 25 years. This is to avoid contributing to the orbital debris Problem. Obviously if the Cubesat mission takes it away from the Earth, either towards the Sun or towards the outer planets, this restriction does not apply. Also, Cubesats delivered to the International Space Station can remain attached to the outside of the station for long periods of time, and be retrieved and returned by a resupply flight.

Propulsion

Generally, Cubesats are not allowed to have a propulsion system. They are specifically constrained to not exhaust any gas, even nitrogen. However, NASA can use propulsion on their own small satellites. Another way for Cubesats to wander the solar system is via solar sails, which use the solar wind, emanating from the Sun, much as a sailboat uses the terrestrial wind. This has been demonstrated by Cubesats.

Flight Dynamics

Flight Dynamics includes the attitude determination and control of the spacecraft. NASA/GSFC's General Mission Analysis Tool (GMAT) is available as free and open source software, under the NASA Open Source Agreement. The tool provides the ability to model and optimize spacecraft trajectories. The domain can be LEO, lunar, interplanetary, or even deep space. This no longer requires a room full of large mainframes, but can be done on a laptop.

The spacecraft has to know its orientation with respect to an inertial frame of reference. We use the word "orbit" to describe the spacecraft's position and velocity. It used to be the case that a separate facility would use the tracking data to calculate the orbital parameters, and forward these to the Control Center. Later, the Control Centers generally took over this function. We need not only the parameters of the orbit as its exists now, but what it will be in the future. This is the function of orbit propagation. We are limited in how far into the future we can predict the orbit, due to data limitations, perturbations that affect the spacecraft, and not having a closed form solution.

If the spacecraft uses magnetic torquer bars to push against the Earth's magnetic field for attitude adjustment or momentum unloading, we need a map of the Earth's magnetic field, particularly, the orientation of magnetic north to "north" in the inertial frame of reference.

Generally, the attitude of a spacecraft is described as a vector in a frame of reference that is body-centered in the spacecraft. We can use three rotational parameters to describe the spacecraft's attitude with respect to this frame. These parameters are generally referred to as roll, pitch, and yaw, derived from aircraft usage. Keep in mind, the body-centric frame we are using is moving with the spacecraft, relative to the Earth Centered frame. We use

Newtonian rigid-body dynamics. This is a good approximation, unless the spacecraft has a lot of fuel onboard, or large solar panels or communication antennae, in which case it does not act as a rigid body.

Roll indicates a rotation about the velocity vector, the direction of motion. *Pitch* is a rotation up and down, with respect to the velocity vector. *Yaw* is a left-right rotation about the velocity vector. It makes more sense in an aircraft, with wings.

There is another entity that is sometimes used for attitude, called quaternions. These are 4-unit vectors (as opposed to the 3-unit roll-pitch-yaw), so they contain redundant information. They are a little easier to calculate, Keep in mind, we can rotate in 2 or 3 directions at the same time. So, quaternions, invented in 1843, are used to calculate and describe complex three dimensional rotations. There is redundant information, but the 4-unt quarternion fits the cache structure better because its a power of 2 elements.

Essentially, the quaternion is a vector in the inertial space, pointing in a direction described by the dimensions along the three axes. Then, a fourth parameter describes a rotation around that vector.

Euler angles are used to describe the rotation of an object with respect to a rigid frame of reference. If we use the spacecraft body-centric frame, the Euler angles correspond to roll, pitch, and yaw.

It is fairly easy to translate from quaternions back and forth to Euler angles. This is left as an exercise for the student.

Standards

There are many Standards applicable to Cubesats. Why should we be interested in standards? Standards represent an established approach, based on best practices. Standards are not created to stifle creativity or dictate an implementation approach, but rather to capture the benefits of previous experience. Adherence to standards implies that different parts will work together. Standards are often developed by a single company, and then adopted by the relevant industry. Other standards are mandated by large customer organizations such as the Department of Defense, or NASA. Many standards organizations exist to develop, review, and maintain standards.

Standards exist in many areas, including hardware, software, interfaces, protocols, testing, system safety, security, and certification. Standards can be open or proprietary.

Hardware standards include the form factor and packaging of chips, the electrical interface, the bus interface, the power interface, and others. The JTAG standard specifies an interface for debugging.

In computers, the Instruction set architecture (ISA) specifies the instruction set. It does not specify the implementation. A popular ISA is ARM (ARM Holdings, LTD), used for Raspberry Pi and Arduino. These are proprietary, and licensed by the Intellectual Property holder to chip manufacturers.

In software, an API (applications program interface) specifies the interface between a user program, and the operating system. To run properly, the program must adhere to the API.
Language standards also exist, such as those for the ANSI c and Java languages. Networking standards include TCP/IP for Ethernet, the CAN bus from Bosch, IEEE-1553 for avionics, and USB.

It is always good to review what standards are available and could be applied to a system, as it ensures the application of best practices from experience, and interoperability with other systems.

PC-104 is an industry for the form factor of embedded computer boards (90 x 96mm) and a motherboard. The standard covers the physical dimensions, power supply type, location of mounting holes, number of ports on the back panel. A lot of Cubesat electronics boards are built to the PC-104 standard.

ARINC 653 is a software specification (API) for space and time partitioning in safety critical real-time operating systems. Each piece of application software has its own memory and dedicated time slot. The specification dates from 1996.

Flight systems electronics usually require MIL-STD-883b, Class-S, radiation-hard (total dose), SEU-tolerant parts. MIL-STD-883 is the standard for testing and screening of parts. Specific issues of radiation tolerance are discussed in MIL-M-38510. Class-S parts are specifically for space-flight use. Because of the need for qualifying the parts for space, the state-of-the-art in spaceborne electronics usually lags that of the terrestrial commercial parts by 5 years.

NASA's standard for parts selection, screening, qualification, and derating is NASA/TP-2003-212242. Download yourself a copy.

The Consultive Committee for Space Data Standards, (CCSDS), maintains International standards that covers system engineering, space link, space-internetworking, and onboard interfaces. The CCSDS is made up of 11 member nations, and over 750 missions have used these standards.

Why don't we just use good old TCP/IP? Transmission Control Protocol/Internet Protocol was designed for terrestrial usage. It assumes end-end connectivity, and low delays. It focuses on speed and simplicity. Space communications can be long-delay. IP assumes seamless, end-end, available data path. Some of the newer mobile IP protocols more closely address the space environment.

The use of Internet Protocol for space missions is a convenience, and piggy-backs on the large established infrastructure of terrestrial data traffic. However, there are problems. A variation of mobile IP is used, because the spacecraft might not always be in view of a ground station, and traffic through the Tracking and Data Relay Satellites involves a significant delay. A hand off scheme between various "cell" sites must be used, and a delay-tolerant protocol.

The formalized Interplanetary Internet evolved from a study at

JPL, lead by Internet pioneer Vint Cerf, and Adrian Hook, from the CCSDS group. The concepts evolved to address very long delay and variable delay in communications links. For example, the Earth to Mars delay varies depending on where each planet is located in its orbit around the Sun. For some periods, one planet is behind the Sun from the point of view of the other, and communications between them is impossible for days and weeks. The Interplanetary Internet implements a Bundle Protocol to address large and variable delays. Normal IP traffic assumes a seamless, end-to-end, available data path, without worrying about the physical mechanism. The Bundle protocol addresses the case of high probability of errors, and disconnections. This protocol was tested in communication with an Earth orbiting satellite in 2008

The CCSDS, Consultive Committee on Space Data Standards, has evolved a delay tolerant protocol for use in space. A concept called the Interplanetary Internet uses a store-and-forward node in orbit around a planet (initially, Mars) that would burst-transmit data back to Earth during available communications windows. At certain times, when the geometry is right, the Mars bound traffic might encounter significant interference. Mars surface craft communicate to Orbiters, which relay the transmissions to Earth. This allows for a lower wattage transmitter on the surface vehicle. Mars does not (yet) have the full infrastructure that is currently in place around the Earth – a network of navigation, weather, and communications satellites.

The Cubesat Space Protocol is a network layer protocol, specifically for Cubesats, released in 2010 It features a 32-bit header with both network layer and transport layer data. It is written in the c language, and works with linux and FreeRTOS. The protocol and its implementation is Open source. At the physical layer, the protocol supports CAN bus, I2C, RS-232, TCP/IP, and CCDSDS space link protocol.

In space, we can use FTP over CCSDS, but watch those NAK's. When you send a packet and receive a negative acknowledgment (NAK), you usually resend. Too many negative acknowledgments can overload the capacity of the link. There is a defined and Interplanetary Internet, which address long delays and major error sources. It uses store-and-forward (like the Internet) nodes in orbit around a planet., such as Mars. It uses burst transmission back to Earth. It is a bundle protocol, and assumes a high probability of errors and a non-continuous link. This is a JPL Project.

Cubesat Onboard Computers

On regular space missions, the use of a Radiation-hardened flight computer is essential. This can be orders of magnitude more expensive that the terrestrial equivalent, and the state of the art lags commercial practice by at least one hardware generation.

Besides the standard 32-bit integer and floating point data structures, the cpu may contain specialized processing units. An example of one of these is the GPU found in the Raspberry Pi.

Graphics Processing Unit (GPU)

A GPU is a specialized computer architecture to manipulate image data at high rates. It can be a single chip, or incorporated with a general purpose CPU. The GPU devices are highly parallel, and specifically designed to handle image data, and operations on that data. They do this much fastest than a programmed general purpose CPU. Most desktop machines have the GPU function on a video card or integrated with their CPU. Originally, GPU's were circuit card based. GPU operations are very memory intensive. The GPU design is customized to (Single Instruction, Multiple Data) SIMD type operations.

The instruction set of the GPU is specific to graphics operations on block data. The requirements were driven by the demands of 2-D and 3-D video games on pc's, phones, tablets, and dedicated gaming units. As GPU units became faster and more capable, they began to consume more power (and thus generate more heat) than the associated CPU's. They are applicable to many classes of Science Data processing.

Although designed to process video data, some GPU's have been used as adjunct data processors and accelerators in other areas involving vectors and matrices, such as the inverse discrete cosine transform. Types of higher-level processing implemented by

GPU's include texture mapping, polygon rendering, object rotation, and coordination system transformation. They also support object shading operations, data oversampling, and interpolation. GPU's find a major application area in video decoding. Building on this, GPU's enable advanced features in digital cameras. These features are supported by Image Processing Libraries. This can be employed in star-tracking cameras, and to facilitate orbit and attitude calculations.

Other specialized processors exist that are optimized for special data structures, and the operations on these data.

Vector Processor

Vector processing involves the processing of vectors of related data, in a (single instruction, multiple data) *SIMD*_mode. For example, vector addition is an SIMD operation.

SIMD refers to a class of parallel computers that perform the same operations on multiple data items simultaneously. This is data level parallelism, which is found in multimedia (video and audio) data used in gaming applications. The SIMD approach evolved from the vector supercomputers of the 1970's, which operated upon a vector of data with a single operation. A popular application of SIMD architecture is Intel's MMX (Multimedia Extensions) instruction set circa 1996 for the X-86 architecture. This feature found its way into the 64-bit ARM implementations.

Digital Signal Processor

Digital signal processors resemble computers in many ways, and come in embedded versions. They handle specialized data types, and include special-purpose operations derived from the digital signal processing realm. This includes the Multiply-and-Add (mac), a digital filtering primitive. Digital signal processing finds application with the processing of audio, photographic, and video data.

A Digital Signal Processor (DSP) is similar to a general purpose CPU, but provides specialized operations for DSP-type operations on specialized data formats. Originally, the DSP function was implemented by software running in a CPU. DSP operations usually have time deadline constraints (hard real time requirements).

Mobile phones and cable modems, to name two examples, drove the development of faster, dedicated hardware units. The first practical commercial product based on a DSP chip was Texas Instrument's Speak-n-Spell toy. Before that, the military applications of sonar and radar data processing drove the technology.

The nature of digital domain signal data and filtering require some unique architectural features. Hardware modulo addressing and bit-reversed addressing is used in digital filtering. Operations on data tend to be SIMD. The *Multiply-Accumulate* primitive is the basis for digital filter implementation. Saturation arithmetic is used to prevent overflow. Both fixed point and floating point data are used. A three-memory Harvard architecture allows simultaneous access of an opcode and two operands.

Multicore chips for DSP are now common. These fast DSP's have enabled new technologies and applications such as software-defined radio.

Some ARM chips such as the Cortex-8 family, and the OMAP3 processors include both a general purpose CPU, and a DSP. The Zynq FPGA has an integral ARM processor, and can form the basis of a Software defined radio unit for onboard use.

COTS

Most university-class Cubesat missions have not used radiation hardened parts, due to their high cost and long lead-time. The use of Non-Space-Rated (NSR), Commercial-Off-The-Shelf (COTS) components components contribute to the 50% failure rate noted in these missions.

Memory

Memory for the Cubesat onboard computer is solid state. It can be volatile or non-volatile. Different types of memory have varying radiation tolerance. Non-volatile memory includes EEProm, flash, magnetorestrictive, and ferroelectric. Most memory is random access, meaning you can read and write any memory item. Some technologies, such as Flash are random access read, but are written in blocks. Some memory technologies "wear out" beyond a certain number of write cycles. Although the number is large, it can be a problem on longer missions. Volatile memory includes static ram and dynamic ram, two different technologies. All are affected by energetic particles.

Arduino

The 32-bit implementation of the ARM-based Arduino architecture is a strong candidate for Cubesat onboard computers. Many implementations feature a real-time clock, which is an add-on item in the Raspberry Pi architecture. A real time clock allows for the implementation of a real-time operating system. Cubesats with Arduinos have flown in orbit. The Arduino mini on the unit from Interorbital systems incorporates a current sensor to indicate a single event upset may have occurred due to radiation. The Arduino architecture has a relatively low tolerance to radiation damage.

There is actually a rad-hard Arduino architecture from Atmel, the AtmegaS128. It features 128 kBytes of flash, 4 kbytes of Eeprom, 4 kbytes of SRAM, 6 PWM channels, 1 analog comparator, 1 I2C interface, 1 SPI interface, 2 UARTS, 1 ADC, a real time clock, JTAG, and a watchdog timer. The device has 6 sleep modes. It is an 8-bit part, running on 3.3 volts, in a 64-lead ceramic package (CQFP). At this writing, there is a 16-week lead time to get the part, which is priced over $600.

The Raspberry Pi

The Raspberry Pi is a small, inexpensive, single board computer based on the ARM architecture. It is targeted to the academic market. It uses the Broadcom BCM2835 system-on-a-chip, which has a 700 MHz ARM processor, a video GPU, and currently 512 M of RAM. It uses an SD card for storage. The Raspberry Pi runs the GNU/linux and FreeBSD operating systems. It was first sold in February 2012. Sales reached ½ million units by the Fall. Due to the open source nature of the software, Raspberry Pi applications and drivers can be downloaded from various sites. It requires a single power supply, and dissipates less than 5 watts. It has USB ports, and an Ethernet controller. It does not have a real-time clock, but one can easily be added. It outputs video in HDMI resolution, and supports audio output. I/O includes 8 general purpose I/O lines, UART, I2C bus, and SPI bus.

The Raspberry Pi design belongs to the Raspberry Pi Foundation in the UK, which was formed to promote the study of Computer Science. The Raspberry Pi is seen as the successor to the original BBC Microcomputer by Acorn, which resulted in the ARM processor. The unit has enough resources to host an operating system such as linux.

Although the Raspberry Pi is not designed to be Rad hard, it showed a surprisingly good radiation tolerance in tests (in references, see Violette). It continued to operate through a dose of 150 krad(Si), with only the loss of USB connectivity.

The Pi Compute Module, up-datable to Pi 2 supports a 10 DOF IMU, an RTC, Analog to digital converters, a real time clock, a dedicated camera port, and supports the communication interfaces I2C, SPI, GPIO, Ethernet, USB.

PiSat

The PiSat is an open source NASA/GSFC design for a "Distributed Mission Test Platform." It represents an ideal platform for prototyping Cubesat Flight software, as well as educational outreach. The PiSat defines the flight computer (ARM), a sensor suite, the enclosure and battery, and the Flight Software. It was developed by NASA/GSFC Code 582, with IRAD funding. It was developed with help from undergraduate student interns.

The Flight Computer is the Raspberry Pi (2 B+), based on the ARM architecture, and running the linux operating system or RTOS, with Code 582's Core Flight System software suite. The supported sensors include a GPS module, magnetometer, compass, accelerometer, a high definition camera, A/D converters, and a real-time clock. Data storage is provided by an SD flash memory card. It uses the Xbee peer-to-peer wireless communication. The price of the hardware components comes in around $350, including the printed enclosure.

Cubesats accept the PC-104 board standard (90 mm x 96 mm), and the boards are stackable. There is no requirement to use this size board, or the standard, but there can be advantages, such as availability of interfaces.

The CFS software will be discussed in detail in the Software section of this document, but we will say here that it is reusable mission software that has already flown on many NASA missions, including the Lunar Reconnaissance Orbiter, and covers common onboard tasks. A collection of applications under the CFS includes uplink and downlink of data, attitude calculation, and support of the camera. There are a set of scripts for startup and shutdown of the system. For test or operations, there are several software choices, including the COSMOS system from Ball Aerospace. The unit is powered via USB during test and development, and by a standard lithium battery for flight.

An intern (and student of the author) integrated a ocean spectrometer into the PiSat architecture at GSFC.

Edison

The Intel Edison board is an emerging competitor to the Arm based boards such as the Arduino and Pi. It uses Intel's x86 architecture. The actual computer module is the size of an SD card.

The second version, from 2014, is 35.5 x 25 mm, with a dual core 500 MHz Atom processor, and a 100 Mhz 32-bit Intel Quark core.

The Quark cpu handles RTOS functions.

The Edison board supports various I/O options including GPIO, USB, SPI, I2C, and PWM. There is a Edison board which is compatible (in a hardware sense) with the Arduino Uno. The Intel Galileo line is a series of x86 architecture "Arduino's." It runs linux, and supports the Arduino "sketches" at the source level.

The Edison has not to my knowledge been tested for radiation hardness,

Other Cubesat CPU Options

If you want guaranteed performance with radiation hardened hardware, it will cost more, but quite a few vendors are available. Here are a few examples.

The NanoMind A712D is an onboard computer for Cubesats. It uses as 32-bit ARM cpu, with 2 megabytes of RAM, and 8 megabytes of flash memory. It can also support a MicroSD flash card. It has a Can bus and a I^{2}C interface. It comes with an extensive software library and real time operating system. Special applications, such as attitude determination and control code are available. It is tolerant to temperatures from -40 to 85 degrees C, but is not completely rad-hard.

The CFC-300 from InnoFlight Inc. of San Diego is another example. It uses the Xilinx Zynq System-on-a-chip architecture. That provides both FPGA capability, and an Arm Cortex A-9 dual core cpu. It has 256 Megabytes of SDRAM, and 32 megabytes of flash. There are multiple synchronous serial interfaces. Daughter cards provide support for SpaceWire, Ethernet, RapidIO, RS-422, and thermistor inputs and heater drive outputs. It can be used with linux or VxWorks.

The Intrepid Cubesat OBC from Tyvak Uses a 400 MHz Atmel processor, and has 128 Mbytes of SDRAM, and 512 Mbytes of flash memory. It draws between 200-300 milliwatts. It includes a command and data handling system, and an onboard electrical power controller. It supports Ethernet, RS-232, USB, and the SPI and I^{2}C interfaces. It includes a JTAG debugging interface. Similar to the Arduino, it supports 3-axis gyros, a 3-axis magnetometer, accelerometers, and a variety of i²c-interfaced sensors. The Microcontroller is an ARM architecture, with digital signal processing extensions. It has a built-in Image Sensor interface.

COVE is JPL's Xilinx Virtex-5 FPGA-based onboard processor for Cubesats. The FPGA is rad-hard. This high end machine provides sufficient power for onboard data processing, while providing a low power mode for periods where the number crunching is not needed. The FPGA can be reconfigured in flight. It has flown in space several times.

The Yaliny flight computer is based on the Microsemi Igloo-2 FPGA SOC. It is inherently SEU-immune. There is a soft processor core, implemented withing the FPGA. It has 8 megabytess of non-volatile, error-correcting memory, and 16 megs of static ram with error-correction. There is the ability to support 1 gigabyte of DDR SDRAM with error correction. It supports the 1553 bus, Ethernet, RS-485 quad pci-express busses, and usb (for debugging). The processor dissipates 2 watts nominally.

The proliferation of low cost and hobbyist grade Flight Computers can only have a positive effect on making the next generation of spacecraft smarter, cheaper, and more capable.

Sensors, Actuators and Mechanisms

This section discusses sensors and actuators on Cubesats. A Cubesat will generally be a sensor platform. It will have a primary mission, but also needs sensors for attitude determination and control, and housekeeping.

Sensors and sensor interfacing

A *sensor* is a device that measures a physical quantity by changing state in response to the stimulation, and producing a signal. It is an analog world. It is rare that we get to interface directly to a digital source. Some sensors may indicate one of two states (presence/absence) with a simple digital signal that may only require voltage level shifting. Other signals, such as a switch closure, may appear digital, but require *debouncing* due to the physics of the actual contact, which actually closes and opens hundreds of times on activation. This is a form of signal conditioning for the sensor. We haven't yet considered voltage levels, current requirements, timing, and all those other real-world interfacing issues. We tend to view sensors as a "black-box" function, where the output is a valid representation of the applied signal. The ugly truth is, sensors are real-world devices that have their own non-linearity, parametric shifts, and they tend to respond to a lot more than the parameter we are interested in.

Some sensors output a digital value that could be sign-magnitude format, 1's complement, 2's complement, Grey code, or some other scheme. The data format might be BCD or binary (signed or unsigned) or something else. The word length may be unique to the sensor, and the data may not come out all at the same time – it might be serial by bit, serial by byte, MSB first, LSB first, etc.

Passive sensors simply collect energy from the sensed phenomena; active sensors require power, or an excitation signal. A *transducer* is a device that converts one form of energy to another; a solar cell is an example. In the literature, the terms sensor and transducer are often used interchangeably.

All sensors are built to operate within a specified environment that corresponds to the temperature limits and other environmental conditions of its applied surroundings. Even if other sensors exist, they may not satisfy all essential conditions to operate within the system, including operating life, sensing range, accuracy, redundancy, low energy consumption, environments, mounting mechanism, reliability, sensing rate with response time, volume, and mass.

It is expected that the software in the embedded processor will sort this all out. With Smart Sensors with integrated processing, more common interface standards between the sensor and the main processor can be applied.

Signal conditioning refers to processing the sensed signal into a form from which the digital processor can then extract useful information. This may involve amplification or attenuation, analog to digital conversion, filtering, format conversion, electrical isolation, and other techniques. Noise filtering is a commonly applied technique. Sensors exhibit lag and hysteresis, which is a difference in offset from one measurement direction to another. Bias refers to the situation when the output is not zero when the measured quantity is. There can be dynamic errors, caused by rapid change in the input. *Drift* refers to the fact that, over time, the sensor may change output while the input remains steady.

The physics of the sensor must be considered. A relative humidity sensor measures relative humidity, but also temperature. A digital compass also reacts to magnetic fields produced by nearby wiring. Sensors are inherently non-linear. All of these characteristics must be understood and compensated for in software or hardware. With smart sensors, this compensation and processing would be accomplished within the sensor unit itself. For a simple sensor unit, some processing and conditioning must be done within the main embedded processor. Consider issues of operating life, range, maximum and minimum, accuracy, redundancy, energy consumption, heat generation, electromagnetic interference generation, electromagnetic interference susceptibility, mounting, reliability, sense rate, transient and steady-state response time, mass and volume, aging, and mean time to failure when choosing sensors.

As an example, the output signal may not vary linearly with the sensed value, and may depend on other ambient conditions as well. A polynomial function in software may need to be applied to the sensed input to generate the correct output. This can be implemented by calculation, or a table look-up.

Between the sensor and the processor, we may need a level of isolation, to protect either or both sides. This might be optical, capacitive, or magnetic in nature. Common grounding is also a concern.

We will examine some real sensors and their physics to see the different characteristics.

Types of Measurement

This section will discuss the types of measurement domains that are typically encountered, and the approaches to sensing and detecting in each.

Voltage

Voltage sensing can involve simple analog to digital circuits, with pre-scaling appropriate to the expected range. The issues of accuracy (8, 12, 16 bits) and conversion time (sample time) apply. The voltage sensor can be operated continuously or on demand. If a simple presence or absence of a specific voltage is desired (is the 3.3 volts present?) a Zener diode circuit can be used. Negative voltages may require the use of op amps to shift the ground to a more convenient place.

Current

Current sensors find application as electronic fuses and circuit breakers. They are also used for current limiting and control in power supplies and motors. Besides the Hall effect magnetic sensor discussed below, resistive current sensors are also used. If the current to be sensed is not direct, but alternating, other methods need to be employed.

Capacitance

Capacitive sensing relies on an external physical parameter changing either the spacing or the dielectric constant between the two plates of a capacitor or affecting the capacitor's salient characteristics. The advantages of capacitive sensing are very low power consumption and relatively good stability of the measurement with temperature.

In a "good" capacitor, a dielectric constant K and the element geometry must be stable throughout the operating environments such as temperature, barometric pressure, humidity, and solvents. These "good capacitors" are essential circuit components in electrical circuits, but if their parameters shift during circuit operation the performance is unacceptable. Conversely, if you want to make a good sensor you need to use a "bad" capacitor, whose parameters varies with the stimuli to be sensed and measured. By the proper choice of materials the capacitive sensor's parameters vary with the environmental stimuli to be differentiated in a predictable and repeatable manner.

Inductive Sensing

The basic principle is related to the inductance change by the position change of the moving element that holds either a ferromagnetic material or an electromagnet. Semiconductor devices such as Hall Effect sensors can detect the inductance change. The measurement method enables the integration of numerous applications including flow sensing, position detection (for example Linear Variable Differential Transformer (LVDT) and Rotational Variable Differential Transformer (RVDT), position rate, angular velocity, and force and torque measurements.

Magnetic field sensing

Magnetic sensing makes use of induction effects, as we move a coil in a magnetic field, or fundamental atomic properties such as Zeeman splitting or nuclear magnetic resonance.

Resistive sensors

These devices have variable resistance in response to particular phenomena. Generally, resistive materials are temperature sensitive, and are also sensitive to moisture.

Temperature and relative humidity sensing

In the simplest case, a precision resistor or semiconductor junction is used, where the current flow is proportional to the ambient temperature. Thermistors are special resistors whose resistance varies with temperature. These devices have to be compensated for self-heating. They are only good over limited ranges. If actual degrees (F or C) are required, the equation is usually a 2nd order polynomial. Relative humidity is usually measured with a capacitive sensor, although conductive polymers with variable resistance are also used. Thermocouples are passive devices, using two dissimilar materials to generate a voltage proportional to the junction temperature. RTD's, resistance temperature detectors, are mostly made of a pure metal or a bulk silicon material.

Sensing at cryogenic temperatures (-150 degrees C or below) is done mostly with resistive sensors. They are very stable once they are temperature stabilized.

Distance, velocity, and acceleration sensing

Distance can be measured with a variety of methods. We can measure direct mechanical motion with a linearly variable resistor or inductor. Velocity is a time difference of distances, and acceleration is a time difference of velocities. The angular distances, velocities, and accelerations are handled just as easily.

Radiant energy sensing and measurement

This includes the spectrum of radio frequency, infrared, optical, ultraviolet, gamma rays, and beyond. The particular sensor technology used depends on the frequency, but the principles are the same.

Thermal detector devices transform a radiant, infrared or thermal transfer energy stimulus into an electrical signal. Most often, the absorbed energy stimuli causes a change in the detectors temperature, and this change in temperature manifests itself as a change in electrical resistance or electrostatic polarization. The sensitivity is limited by the fluctuation in energy of the absorbed energy.

The measurement of radiant energy has many applications. The choice of the measuring device depends on the frequency range of the energy and the particular application location or structure. Thermal detectors include thermocouples, bolometers, thermal imaging devices, resistance-temperature devices such as doped germanium and silicon cells, optical pyrometers, photoconductive cells and photoelectric cells, voltage-current devices such as a thermistor, Seebeck Effect devices or RTD. Some of these radiant energy detectors require special operating temperatures.

Photodetectors are semiconductor devices that can detect optical signals through electronic processes. Quantum photodetectors are nonequlibrium devices. A minimum amount of photon energy is required to create a quantum excitation; this is referred to as a photo-absorption threshold. The photodetector output signal depends on the non-equlibrium between excitation and recombination in the semiconductor crystal lattice. The signal amplitude is directly dependent on the photo-excitation lifetime and the number of absorbed photons.

Types of sensors

This section will discuss the application of the laws of physics and materials properties to real-world sensors.

MEMS accelerometer

The *MEMS*, or micro electro mechanical system, uses a chip-level integrated circuit technology to provide measurement devices. The advantage is that the sensors are made in processes developed for semiconductor manufacturer, and are inexpensive to mass-produce.

A typical accelerometer sensor has a small gas-filled chamber with a center heating element, and four temperature sensors around the edge. A static sensor results in all four temperature elements reading the same value. As the sensor is tilted, the higher sensor will read hotter. The sensor itself translates temperature differences into pulse widths. Some trigonometric calculations are needed to resolve angles. It also does not work in zero G, due to the lack of convection currents, which require gravity.

These sensors can be used to determine acceleration, tilt, rotation, vibration, and other derived values.

Piezo Accelerometer

In a piezo-electric accelerometer, a mass exerts force on a piezo electric element, which generates a charge proportional to the force. The charge is amplified at the sensor. These devices have a characteristic resonant frequency, which is typically much higher than what is expected to be measured. These sensors can operate in compression or shear mode.

Light sensing – intensity

A simple photodiode can be used to distinguish between dark and light. Different spectral sensitivities, perhaps used with filers, can provide color discrimination in the measurement as well. Photodetectors can function as variable resistors, or generators of electricity.

Laser rangefinder/lidar

The *lidar* unit is a light-based analog to radar. With sophisticated processing, it can be used to build a range-map of its surroundings. Depending on the environment and the nature of the sensed object, the lidar can operate in the infrared, visible, or ultraviolet spectrum. Lessons learned from radar can be applied to lidar signal processing. A narrow beam width gives enhanced spatial discrimination. Lidars use a series of movable mirrors to provide 3-dimensional scans in the side-side and up-down directions. Solid-state laser modules are cheap and mass produced. Lidar units are usually smart sensors, including their own internal processing, and produce large volumes of data.

Thermocouple

A *thermocouple* is a thermoelectric contact sensor. Two dissimilar conductors convert the thermal energy directly into electrical energy and two junctions of these conductors are necessary (refer to Seebeck effect). When different segments of the thermocouple are at different temperatures, creating a thermal gradient, from each other an electrical voltage proportional to the temperature difference is maintained in the thermocouple circuit. A thermocouple is a passive sensor meaning it generates voltage in response to temperature differences, and does not require any external electrical excitation power. The voltage produced depends on the temperature gradient between the two thermocouple junctions, regardless of the absolute temperature of each junction. Therefore, if an absolute temperature is required for reference purposes, an RTD or thermistor is required. Thermocouples are capable of being used to directly measure temperatures up to 2600° C.

Thermistor

Thermistors are resistors whose resistance varies with temperature. They can have a positive or negative coefficient. The advantage of a thermistor is that their resistance is usually several orders of magnitude greater than the resistance of the remainder of the circuit. The circuit line resistance therefore has no significant effect on the signal accuracy. A Wheatstone bridge architecture can be used. The thermistor is affected by self-heating. The thermistor was developed by Michael Faraday in 1833.

Piezoelectric Temperature Sensors

These are active sensors whose resistance varies with temperature. The temperature sensor function is based upon the variability of the crystal oscillation frequency at different temperatures. Thermal coupling of the object to be sensed with the oscillating plate of the sensor is often difficult. All piezoelectric temperature sensors have a relatively slow response as compared with thermistor and RTD's or PRT's.

Positive Resistance Thermometers (PRT).

Sometimes called Resistance Thermometer Devices (RTD) or Platinum Resistance Thermometers (PRT), these are temperature sensors that use the predictable change in electrical resistance of some materials subsequent to a corresponding change in temperature. The PRT operates on the principle that the material's electrical resistance changes in a predictable way depending on the rise and fall in temperature. A typical RTD consists of a fine platinum wire wrapped around a mandrel and covered with a protective coating. Usually, the mandrel and coating are glass or ceramic. Wire types consist of a coil of wire which provides a compromise between mechanical stability and allows thermal expansion of the wire but at the expense of mechanical rigidity and strength under mechanical shock and vibration. Film types consist of a thin layer of platinum on a substrate. Due to its small size the device can respond quickly to temperature changes. The Seebeck effect can cause erroneous reading in PRT's.

Strain gage sensors

Strain gage sensors have the attributes of a variable resistor under compressive or tensile strain. They are designed for maximum resistance change due to mechanical strain variations but minimum resistance change in response to other properties such as thermal. The strain gage is manufactured with a thin flexible backing; this enhances ease of handling and installing on the structural or mechanical surface to be strain monitored. As the structure is deformed by either compressive or tensile strain, the resistive element is deformed, causing its electrical resistance to change respectively. This resistance change, usually measured using a Wheatstone bridge, is directly proportional to the surface strain on the structure being monitored.

Gyros

A *gyroscope* is a device for measuring or maintaining orientation, based on the principles of angular momentum. Mechanically, a gyroscope is a spinning wheel or disk in which the axle is free to assume any orientation. Although this orientation does not remain fixed, it changes in response to an external torque much less and in a different direction than it would without the large angular momentum associated with the disk's high rate of spin and moment of inertia. Since external torque is minimized by mounting the device in gimbals, its orientation remains nearly fixed, regardless of any motion of the platform on which it is mounted. The force at the gimbals can be measured with strain gages. An electric motor, or an air motor maintains the gyroscope's rotation rate.

Gyroscopes can also be electronic, microchip-packaged MEMS devices found in consumer electronic devices such as cell phones and video games, solid-state ring lasers, or fiber optics. These do not use a rotating mass.

Applications of gyroscopes include inertial navigation systems where magnetic compasses would not work or would not be precise enough, and for the stabilization of flying vehicles like radio-controlled helicopters, unmanned aerial vehicles, or drone aircraft.

The problem with gyros is their drift with time. The gyro's advantage is continuous output and they are not constrained by the need for an external reference.

Charge Transfer Devices (CTD)

The *CTD*'s used in imaging and sensing correspond to shift registers where the data in the register are analog samples. This enables the device to process analog data without first translating the signal into the digital domain, reducing component count and eliminates the need for analog-to-digital converters. A CTD is basically an array of closely spaced sensor diodes. The operation of a CTD requires charge signal injection, transfer, and readout, under the application of a proper sequence of clock voltage. This pulses the diode array so the charge can be stored and transferred in a controlled manner. These sensor arrays are commonly found in digital cameras.

Magneto-resistive sensors consist of a magneto-resistive thin film deposited on an insulating substrate. The film is then etched into segments to form the sensor network. The resulting segments are interconnected forming the sensor cells. These magneto-resistive sensors are often used to measure rotational speeds, much like a tachometer, or may be used for either incremental or absolute magnetic encoders.

Optical Incremental encoders consist of a disc divided up into alternate optically opaque and transparent sectors, which is driven by the input shaft. A light source is positioned at one side of the disc and a light detector at the other side. As the disc rotates the output from the detector will switch alternately on and off depending on whether an opaque or transparent sector is between the light source and the detector. A stream of square wave pulses is produced which indicate the angular position of the shaft. Most incremental encoders feature a second light source and detector, the output of which is phased in such a way in relation to the main detector output, that the direction of the input shaft can be determined. Many encoders also feature a third light source and detector which acts as a once per revolution index marker. Usually, a Grey-code pattern is used, giving one and only one bit change per position change.

While this type of encoder may be useful in some applications it has the disadvantage of having the angular information stored in an external counter. If the information in this counter is lost (for example if the power supply was temporarily interrupted), there is no way of knowing the shaft angle. Also at initial turn on, there is no way of determining the absolute shaft angle until it has been rotated through the index marker.

Tachometers are often used to measure the rotational speed of a spinning object. Some tachometers utilize LED's in conjunction with optical encoders. Other tachometer types consist of a wheel mounted magnet and a fixed sensor like a pickoff coil. The pulse train may be converted to a DC voltage for error signals for a command variable speed feedback network or constant speed determination. Another type of tachometer uses the back EMF generated by the motor armature to produce an analog voltage proportional to the rotational speed.

Absolute encoders

The loss of angular position information in optical encoders can be overcome by the absolute optical encoder. In this device, the disc is divided up into N sectors, each sector also being divided up along its length into opaque and transparent sections forming a digital word with a maximum count of N. The sectors are arranged such that the digital word formed by each set of opaque and transparent sections, increments in value from one sector to the next. A set of N light sources are arranged radially on one side of the disc and corresponding detectors are positioned on the other side such that a parallel word representing the input shaft angle can be obtained at any one of N angular positions.

Pyroelectric detectors consist of a thin slab of crystal, such as triglycine sulfate, sandwiched between two electrodes. Impinging radiation raises the temperature of the crystal, causes spontaneous charge polarization of the crystal material and yields a measurable potential difference across the electrodes.

Compass module

A compass sensor measures the direction of a prevailing magnetic field. If you are on a planet with a good magnetic field (such as Earth), you can use this sensor to determine bearing with respect to magnetic north. This gives a heading reading, the angle with respect to magnetic north. A change in this reading can be used for rotation rate. Trigonometric functions are required in these calculations. Hall effect electronic sensors can also detect and measure magnetic fields. Fluxgate sensors use a set of coils on a core, with associated excitation circuitry. They have a resolution in the milli-gauss range. They are low cost, but have a slow response time. Magneto-restrictive sensors can be mass-produced as an integrated circuit, and have response times on the order of milliseconds, making them more applicable to moving systems.

The Earth's field is about 0.5 gauss. In the case of Earth, the magnetic field is approximately a dipole field. The components of the field parallel to the local surface are used to determine compass direction. The angle of the field relative to the surface is called the inclination, and varies across the surface. True north and magnetic north vary by up to 25 degrees, true north being the rotational axis of the Earth.

Optical incremental encoder (quadrature encoder)

An incremental rotary encoder provides information about the instantaneous position of a rotating shaft. It does this by producing one square wave cycle per increment of shaft movement. This increment is referred to as the resolution of the encoder and is built directly into the internal hardware of the device. A resolution of 360 means that 360 square wave cycles will be produced in one complete rotation of the shaft. By counting the number of cycles, one can tell the position of the shaft, relative to its starting position. For example, 90 cycles means that the shaft is now at a position 90 degrees from where it started. By adding a quadrature signal, we can measure the direction of the rotation, by reading which signal (A or B) we saw first. By starting a counter with the rising edge of one signal, and stopping it with the trailing edge, we can get very accurate position measurements. Often a Zero signal is added so that the baseline zero position can be known.

Star Sensors

Star sensors measure star coordinates in a spacecraft frame of reference and provide attitude information when these observed coordinates are compared with known star directions obtained from a star catalog. Star sensors can achieve accuracies in the arc-second range. Most star sensors consist of a Sunshade, an optical system, an image definition device which defines the region of the field of view that is visible to the detector, the detector and an electronic assembly. The detector such as a photomultiplier transforms the optical signal into an electrical signal. Solid-state detectors may be noisier than photomultipliers. The electronics assembly amplifies and filters the electrical signal from the detector. If the amplified optical signal from the detector is above a fixed signal intensity, an output is generated signifying the star's presence.

A charge transfer device star sensor is an optical system consisting of a digitally scanned array of photosensitive elements whose output is fed to an embedded microprocessor. A charge pattern corresponding to the received image of the star field viewed is produced. The charge pattern is then read out serially line-by-line to an analog to digital converter and this subsequent signal is stored in memory.

A series of off-the-shelf star trackers for Cubesats are the Blue Canyon Technologies' Nano Star Trackers. They can detect stars to magnitude 7, and include an onboard star catalog with more than 20,000 entries. They require around 1.5 watts.

Magnetometers

Magnetometers measure the induced current in a coil by a planet's magnetic field. This works well at Earth, where the magnetic field has been well mapped. For planets with little or no magnetic field, such as Mars, magnetometers are not very useful. A more sensitive measurement is made with a fluxgate. A fluxgate magnetometer consists of a small, magnetically susceptible core wrapped by two coils of wire. An alternating electric current is passed through one coil, driving the core through an alternating cycle of magnetic saturation. This constantly changing field induces an electric current in the second coil, and this output current is measured by a detector. In a magnetically neutral background, the input and output currents will match. When the core is exposed to a background magnetic field, it will be more easily saturated in alignment with that field and less easily saturated in opposition to it. The induced output current, will be out of step with the input current. The extent to which this happens depends on the strength of the magnetic field.

The normal spacecraft residual magnetism, and generated electromagnetic fields from the operation of electrical equipment interfere with the sensitive magnetometers.

Earth Sensor

An Earth sensor, or, in the generally case, a planetary sensor, can distinguish the warmth of a planet and the cool of deep space. It is generally a scanning instrument, which sees two interface points. It can then determine the center of the planet. This is useful if the science payload wants to look down. One problem that can be encountered is, for the viewpoint of the spacecraft, a solar or lunar eclipse. In the solar eclipse, the planet gets between the spacecraft and the sun. As the sun becomes visible, it "blinds" the earth sensor. Most of these units are self-protecting, and shut down when bright light is detected. During this period of time, the sensor data is not available.

In another curious case that I participated in, our Earth viewing spacecraft seemed to indicate that Earth got bigger. It took a while to figure out that it was a lunar eclipse, from the spacecraft's viewpoint – the moon was visible on the side of the Earth. Momentary panic followed by shrewd deduction.

GPS
The GPS in-orbit satellite-based navigation can be used by satellites below the GPS spacecraft orbit (at 12,600 miles) for time and position services. Generally, four GPS satellites must be in view simultaneously. Commercial off-the-shelf rad-hard fps products for spacecraft are available. This, of course, assumes the planet you are in orbit about has a constellation of GPS satellites. Only Earth has this, so far. Also, there is some software modification required for GPS units that are intended for surface usage. This involves removing the ionosphere correction included in those models.

Actuator and Mechanism Interfacing

Mechanisms require controlled electrical power, and almost always include sensor feedback. A one-time mechanism might be used during deployment. Reaction wheels may be incorporated to maintaining pointing. Antennas and solar arrays may need to be pointed. We have to consider the materials properties including stability in the space environment.

An actuator as we use it here means an electrical to mechanical transducer. This includes motors and solenoids.

Piezoelectric actuators are inherently linear, as solenoids. Standard mechanical mechanisms can be used to convert linear to rotary motion, or vice versa. An actuator may also be used to clamp an object to prevent motion. Actuators are usually classified by their efficiency.

Analog and power interfacing

In a direct current motor, dc is applied to both stator and rotor, or the rotor is a permanent magnet. If there are rotor connections, these must be by slip ring and brushes to allow rotation.

Pulse width modulation control is typically used for motor speed control. In this scheme, the width of a pulse determines the duty cycle of the motor, from 0 to 100%. The pulse repetition rate must be greater than the motor's inertia will allow it to respond to. Typically, this works well with 1 kilohertz, although systems up to 100 KHz are used. During the period of time when the pulse is not active, the back-emf (electro-magnetic force) of the motor can be measured as an indicator of load, and the next pulse adjusted accordingly.

Servos

By definition, a *servomechanism* is an automatic device with feedback. The first may have been James Watt's steam engine speed governor. Earlier, windmills had mechanical speed regulators and wind direction adjusters. Feedback is used to reduce system error. A modern example would be an automotive cruise control system.

The servo system may control position, velocity, acceleration, and angular variations for these quantities, temperature, or other physical parameters.

Today, small servo systems developed for model aircraft and cars are cheap and plentiful. These normally use radio links as a control mechanism. The system consists of an electric motor and a variable resistor for position feedback. The radio link sends a PWM signal, where the width of the pulse indicates a position command. The feedback allows the servo to hold the commanded point. The standard servos used in radio controlled models use a 50-Hertz frame rate. Each pulse has a 20-millisecond width. Servos can be hardwired to the controller as well.

The actual mechanism may be capable of 90, 180, or possibly 360-degree rotation. The system was originally developed as analog (continuous), but is now digital (discrete). Interfaces between servo systems and standard computer interfaces such as USB are available.

Solenoids

Solenoids are linear motion devices using a coil and magnet. They are used for actuating valves, for example. They require a simple application of voltage for operation. Working against a spring, a fairly accurate position can be maintained, at the cost of continuously applied current.

Attitude control can take the form of reaction wheels, where a small mass is spun rapidly, and the large structure of the spacecraft moves in the opposite direction, preserving momentum. Reaction wheels use electrical motors. One problems occurs when there are biases that cause the reaction wheel to saturate in one direction. It must then be unloaded of momentum by reaction jet firing (involving electrically controlled valves), or torquer bars, which, when energized, push against the planet's magnetic field. Electric propulsion, or pulsed plasma propulsion can also be used to make attitude and orbit correction.

Another passive approach is to include a permanent magnet in the Cubesat, which will align the satellite to the Earth's magnetic field.

Spacecraft housekeeping tasks

Besides attitude determination and control, the onboard embedded systems has a variety of housekeeping tasks to attend to.

Generally, there is a dedicated unit, sometimes referred to as the Command & Data Handler (C&DH) with interfaces with the spacecraft transmitters and receivers, the onboard data system, and the flight computer. The C&DH, itself a computer, is in charge of uplinked data (generally, commands), onboard data storage, and data transmission. The C&DH can send received commands directly to various spacecraft components, or can hold them for later dissemination at a specified time. The C&DH has a direct connection with the science instrument(s) for that data stream. If the science instrument package has multiple sensors, there may be a separate science C&DH (SC&DH) that consolidates the sensed data, and hands it over to the C&DH for transmission to the ground. The C&DH can hand over all commands related to science instruments to the IC&DH.

The spacecraft computer calculates and maintains a table of consumables data, both value and usage rate. This includes available electrical power in the batteries, state-of-charge, the amount of thruster propellant remaining, and the status of any other renewable or consumable asset. This is periodically telemetered to the ground. Over the long term, we can do trending on this data, which can help us identify pending problems.

The spacecraft electronics needs to be kept within a certain temperature for proper operation. Generally, the only heat source is the Sun, and the only heat sink is deep space. There are options as to how the spacecraft can be oriented. In close orbit to a planet, the planet may also represent a heat source. Automatic thermal louvers can be used to regulate the spacecraft internal temperature, if they are pointed to deep space. The flight computer's job is to keep the science instrument or communications antennae pointed in the right direction. This might be overridden in case the spacecraft is getting too hot or too cold.

The Flight Computer needs to know the state-of-charge (SOC) of the batteries at all times, and whether current is flowing into or out of the batteries. It the SOC is getting too low, some operations must be suspended, so the solar panels or spacecraft itself can be re-oriented to maximize charging. In some cases, redundant equipment may be turned off, according to a predetermined electrical load-shedding algorithm. If the spacecraft batteries are fully discharged, it is generally the end of the mission, because pointing to the Sun cannot be achieved, except by lucky accident. Don't bet on it.

The spacecraft communications antennae can be pointed to the large antennae of the groundstation. We might just use an omnidirectional antenna, or point the entire spacecraft. Steerable antennas are used in larger spacecraft. The antennae can usually be steered in two axis, independently of the spacecraft body. This can be accomplished in the flight computer.

Safe Hold mode

As a last resort, the spacecraft should have a safe-hold or survival mode that operates without computer intervention. This usually seeks to orient the spacecraft with its solar panels to the Sun to maximize power, turns off all non-essential systems, and calls for help. This can be implemented in a dedicated digital unit. It used to be the case that the safe-hold mode was implemented in analog circuitry.

Power Concerns, and the Cost of Computation

Generally, the computer hardware can be designed to minimize the amount of power it consumes. The next issue is to control the amount of power the software takes.

Power is a constrained resource onboard the spacecraft, and must be carefully managed. We generally have rechargeable batteries, and solar arrays for a power source. The computer has to monitor and control the state-of-charge of the batteries, sometimes dropping everything else it is doing to charge the batteries.

We also have to consider the power usage of the computer, while executing programs. Most embedded cpu's have some power saving modes, that come in handy for your cellphone, for example. These modes have names like "sleep" and "standby." The manufacturers' data sheet will define these modes, and their power consumption, compared to normal operation. In addition, some computers can selectively shut down some memory or I/O resources to reduce power as well.

To control power usage, we first need to add instrumentation to measure it. The embedded processor needs to be able to monitor its own power consumption. On the test bench, we can establish the energy required to run an algorithm. From this data, we make decisions according to the current situation and state as to the correct approach to apply. What we have measured and computed is the energy cost of computation.

Let's look at a simple example of onboard data processing on a small satellite imaging mission. Here we are taking consecutive images at a resolution of 5 megapixels. This is 40 megabits, at 8 bits per pixel. In Cubesats, you have a limited downlink bandwidth due to power issues, and you only have communications over land. Cubesat generally do not have the resources to utilize the Tracking and Data Relay Satellites at a higher orbit. This implies we need to know when we are over land. There are lots of ways to do this, but we could run a simple orbit model onboard with stored maps. The spacecraft takes images continuously, stores them onboard, and downlinks them when a receiver is available.

We could also consider doing some image processing onboard. The Raspberry Pi, Model B 2, for example has an Image Processing pipeline separate from the main cpu cores. It is supported by an open source image processing library. We can implement various levels of data compressing on the image, or do image differencing, or process to only include "areas of interest." All of this is feasible, but involves a lot of computation, which, in turn, uses a lot of power. So, we might consider only doing the computations, on stored data, when the Cubesat is in sunlight. We can predict this, and it is relatively easy to sense.

We might run into a conflict between processing the images, and downlinking them, if the Cubesat is in sunlight, and over land. A housekeeping task for an onboard computer is to keep track of the state-of-charge of the battery's by measuring current in and current out.

Open Source

This is a topic we need to discuss before we go into software. It is not a technical topic, but concerns your right to use (and/or own, modify) software. It's those software licenses you click to agree with, and never read. That's what the intellectual property lawyers are betting on.

Software and software tools are available in proprietary and open source versions. Open source software is free and widely available, and may be incorporated into your system. It is available under license, which generally says that you can use it, but derivative products must be made available under the same license. This presents a problem if it is mixed with purchased, licensed commercial software, or a level of exclusivity is required. Major government agencies such as the Department of Defense and NASA have policies related to the use of Open Source software.

Adapting a commercial or open source operating system to a particular problem domain can be tricky. Usually, the commercial operating systems need to be used "as-is" and the source code is not available. The software can usually be configured between well-defined limits, but there will be no visibility of the internal workings. For the open source situation, there will be a multitude of source code modules and libraries that can be configured and customized, but the process is complex. The user can also write new modules in this case.

Large corporations or government agencies sometimes have problems incorporating open source products into their projects. Open Source did not fit the model of how they have done business traditionally. They are issues and lingering doubts. Many Federal agencies have developed Open Source policies. NASA has created an open source license, the NASA Open Source Agreement (NOSA), to address these issues.

It has released software under this license, but the Free Software Foundation had some issues with the terms of the license. The Open Source Initiative (OpenSource.org) maintains the definition of Open Source, and certifies licenses such as the NOSA. (HTTP://opensource.org/licenses/NASA-1.3) The GNU General Public License (GPL) is the most widely used free software license. It guarantees end users the freedoms to use, study, share, copy, and modify the software. Software that ensures that these rights are retained is called free software. The license was originally written by Richard Stallman of the Free Software Foundation (FSF) for the GNU project in 1989. The GPL is a *copyleft* license, which means that derived works can only be distributed under the same license terms. This is in distinction to permissive free software licenses, of which the BSD licenses are the standard examples. Copyleft is in counterpoint to traditional copyright. Proprietary software "poisons" free software, and cannot be included or integrated with it, without abandoned the GPL. The GPL covers the GNU/linux operating systems and most of the GNU/linux-based applications.

A Vendor's software tools and operating system or application code is usually proprietary intellectual property. It is unusual to get the source code to examine, at least without binding legal documents and additional funds. Along with this, you do get the vendor support. An alternative is open source code, which is in the public domain. There are a series of licenses covering open source code usage, including the Creative Commons License, the gnu public license, copyleft, and others. Open Source describes a collaborative environment for development and testing. Use of open source code carries with it an implied responsibility to "pay back" to the community. Open Source is not necessarily free.

The Open source philosophy is sometimes at odds with the rigidized procedures evolved to ensure software performance and reliability. Offsetting this is the increased visibility into the internals of the software packages, and control over the entire software package. Besides application code, operating systems such as GNU/linux and bsd can be open source. The programming language Python is open source. The popular web server Apache is also open source.

A list of open source tools for Cubesats can be found here:

http://wiki.developspace.net/Open_Source_Engineering_Tools

Examples include a Java-based astrodynamics tool, tools for

Mission Analysis, orbit determination and prediction, spacecraft simulation and modeling, a satellite constellation visualizer, a tool for solar sails, and more. As will be discussed later on in this book, a complete open source control center is available. This is the COSMOS product from Ball Aerospace. The author has direct hands-on experience implementing a Cubesat control center, on a laptop, using this toolset.

The JAVA Astrodynmaics Toolkit(JAT) on Sourceforge. JAT is a is a library of components to help users create their own application programs to solve problems in Astrodynamics, mission design, spacecraft navigation, guidance and control using Java or Matlab. It is not an application program, although there are a number of example programs included. You have to be able to write Java or Matlab programs to use JAT.

Example programs are available to demonstrate the capabilities of JAT as well as to allow new users to quickly learn how to make use of the built-in features of JAT.

From their website:

"After using COTS Astrodynamics software, we have learned that no one application can satisfy all the needs of a researcher in the field of Astrodynamics. Therefore, we decided that JAT should be a software component library so that the users could have flexibility to create their own applications. However, since we are asking users to develop their own applications, the software components must be easy to integrate and use."

One choice of the programming language is Java.

Features

- Astrodynamics constants
- Time transformations
- Coordinate transformations
- Quaternions
- Orbit element conversions

- Gravity models: Two-body, Restricted three body problem, JGM-3
- Attitude Dynamics
- Third body effects due to sun and moon
- Atmospheric drag models: Harris-Priester density model
- Solar radiation pressure
- Lambert Problem
- Kepler Equation solver
- Accurate orbit propagation
- Integrators: fixed and adaptive step-size Runge-Kutta
- JPL Ephemerides
- Linear equation solver
- Unconstrained optimization (BFGS)
- Non-linear equation solvers, including Newton-Raphson and Regula Falsi
- Linear Algebra (based on JAMA and JMAT)
- Ground Tracks
- 3-D Visualization for orbits and trajectories
- GPS, INS and integrated GPS/INS simulation

Open source can also apply to electronics and computers, besides software. It's a definition of your rights concerning ownership and usage.

ITAR

Systems that provide "satellite control software" are included under the International Trafficking in Arms (ITAR) regulation, as the software is defined as "munitions" subject to export control. The Department of State interprets and enforces ITAR regulations. It applies to items that might go to non-US citizens, even citizens of friendly nations or NATO Partners. Even items received from Allies may not necessarily be provided back to them. Software and embedded systems related to launch vehicles and satellites are given particular scrutiny. The ITAR regulations date from the period of the Cold War with the Soviet Union. Increased enforcement of ITAR regulations recently have resulted in American market share in satellite technology declining. A license is required to export controlled technology. This includes passing technical information to a foreign national within the United States. Penalties of up to $100 million have been imposed for violations of the ITAR Regulations, and imprisonment is also possible. Something as simple as carrying ITAR information on a laptop or storage medium outside the US is considered a violation. ITAR regulations are complex, and need to be understood when working in areas of possible application. ITAR regulations apply to the hardware, software, and Intellectual Property assets, as well as test data and documentation.

Onboard Software

Flight s/w is a special case of embedded software. As such, it is generally more difficult to design, implement, and test. It must be treated carefully, because most of the Cubesat functionality will rely on software, and the mission success will be directly related to software.

Flight Software can be proprietary or Open Source, but almost all Cubesat onboard software is open source.

FSW has several distinguishing characteristics:

- There are no direct user interfaces such as monitor and keyboard. All interactions are through uplink and downlink.

- It interfaces with numerous flight hardware devices such as thrusters, reaction wheels, star trackers, motors, science instruments, temperature sensors, etc.

- It executes on radiation-hardened processors and microcontrollers that are relatively slow and memory-limited.

- It performs real-time processing. It must satisfy numerous timing constraints (timed commands, periodic deadlines, async event response). Being late = being wrong.

- Besides attitude determination and control, the onboard embedded systems has a variety of housekeeping tasks to attend to.

NASA's Core Flight Executive, and Core Flight Software

The Core Flight Executive, from the Flight Software Branch at NASA/GSFC, is an open source operating system framework. The executive is a set of mission independent reusable software services and an operating environment. Within this architecture, various mission-specific applications can be hosted. The cFE focuses on the commonality of flight software. The Core Flight System (CFS) supplies libraries and applications. Much flight software legacy went into the concept of the cFE. It has gotten traction within the Goddard community, and is in use on many flight projects, simulators, and test beds
(FlatSats) at multiple NASA centers.

The cFE presents a layered architecture, starting with the bootstrap process, and including a real time operating system. At this level, a board support package is needed for the particular hardware in use. Many of these have been developed. At the OS abstraction level, a Platform support package is included. The cFE core comes next, with cFE libraries and specific mission libraries. Ap's habituate the 5_{th}, or upper layer. The cFE strives to provide a platform and project independent run time environment.

The boot process involves software to get things going after power-on, and is contained in non-volatile memory. cFE has boot loaders for the RAD750 (from BAE), the Coldfire, and the Leon3 architecture. The real time operating systems can be any of a number of different open source or proprietary products, VxWorks and RTEMS for example. This layer provides interrupt handling, a scheduler, a file system, and interprocess communication.

The Platform Support Package is an abstraction layer that allows the cFE to run a particular RTOS on a particular hardware platform. There is a PSP for desktop pc's for the cFE. The cFE Core includes a set of re-usable, mission independent services. It presents a standardized application Program Interface (API) to the programmer. A software bus architecture is provided for messaging between applications.

The Event services at the core level provides an interface to send asynchronous messages, telemetry. The cFE also provides time services.

Aps include a Health and Safety Ap with a watchdog. A housekeeping AP for messages with the ground, data storage and file manager aps, a memory checker, a stored command processor, a scheduler, a checksummer, and a memory manager. Aps can be developed and added to the library with ease.

A recent NASA/GSFC Cubesat project uses a FPGA-based system on a chip architecture with Linux and the cFE. CFE and its associated cFS are available as an architecture for Cubesats in general.

The cFE has been released into the World-Wide Open Source community, and has found many applications outside of NASA.

NASA's software Architecture Review Board reviewed the cFE in 2011. They found it a well thought-out product that definitely met a NASA need. It was also seen to have the potential of becoming a dominant flight software architectural framework. The technology was seen to be mature.

The cFS is the core flight software, a series of aps for generally useful tasks onboard the spacecraft. The cFS is a platform and project independent reusable software framework and set of reusable applications. This framework is used as the basis for the flight software for satellite data systems and instruments, but can be used on other embedded systems in general. More information on the cFS can be found at http://cfs.gsfc.nasa.gov/OSAL

The OS Abstraction Layer (OSAL) project is a small software

library that isolates the embedded software from the real time operating system. The OSAL provides an Application Program Interface (API) to an abstract real time operating system. This provides a way to develop one set of embedded application code that is independent of the operating system being used. It is a form of middleware.

cFS aps

CFS aps are core Flight System (CFS) applications that are plug-in's to the Core Flight Executive (cFE) component. Some of these are discussed below.

CCSDS File Delivery (CF)

The CF application is used for transmitting and receiving files. To transfer files using CFDP, the CF application must communicate with a CFDP compliant peer. CF sends and receives file information and file-data in Protocol Data Units (PDUs) that are compliant with the CFDP standard protocol defined in the CCSDS 727.0-B-4 Blue Book. The PDUs are transferred to and from the CF application via CCSDS packets on the cFE's software bus middleware.

Limit check (LC)

The LC application monitors telemetry data points in a cFS system and compares the values against predefined threshold limits. When a threshold condition is encountered, an event message is issued and a Relative Time Sequence (RTS) command script may be initiated to respond/react to the threshold violation.

Checksum (CS)

The CS application is used for for ensuring the integrity of onboard memory. CS calculates Cyclic Redundancy Checks (CRCs) on the different memory regions and compares the CRC values with a baseline value calculated at system start up. CS has the ability to ensure the integrity of cFE applications, cFE tables, the cFE core, the onboard operating system (OS), onboard EEPROM, as well as, any memory regions ("Memory") specified by the users.

Stored Command (SC)
The SC application allows a system to be autonomously commanded 24 hours a day using sequences of commands that are loaded to SC. Each command has a time tag associated with it, permitting the command to be released for distribution at predetermined times. SC supports both Absolute Time tagged command Sequences (ATSs) as well as multiple Relative Time tagged command Sequences (RTSs).

Scheduler (SCH)
The SCH application provides a method of generating software bus messages at predetermined timing intervals. This allows the system to operate in a Time Division Multiplexed (TDM) fashion with deterministic behavior. The TDM major frame is defined by the Major Time Synchronization Signal used by the cFE TIME Services (typically 1 Hz). The Minor Frame timing (number of slots executed within each Major Frame) is also configurable.

File Manager (FM)
The FM application provides onboard file system management services by processing ground commands for copying, moving, and renaming files, decompressing files, creating directories, deleting files and directories, providing file and directory informational telemetry messages, and providing open file and directory listings. The FM requires use of the cFS application library.

Rad-Hard Software

The major problem for Spaceflight computers is radiation, although there are other environmental issues, and there can always be hardware and software residual errors that made it through testing

Rad Hard software is an approach that is software-based, and running on the system it is testing. From formal testing results, and with certain key engineering tools, we can come up with likely failure modes, and possible remediations. Besides self-test, we can have cross-checking of systems. Not everything can be tested by the software, without some additional hardware. First we will discuss the engineering analysis that will help us define the possible hardware and software failure cases, and then we will discuss possible actions and remediations. None is this is new, but the suggestion is to collect together best practices in the software testing area, develop a library of RHS routines, and get operational experience. These routines will be open source.

Another advantage of the software approach is that we can change it after launch, as more is learned, and conditions change.

This section explores an approach to detect and respond to pending radiation damage to flight computers.

The RHS has many diverse pieces, and is not just one software module, but can be dispersed. Some of the RHS modules run continuously and some are triggered on demand, due to a specific event. It is desirable to have as much fault/failure coverage as possible, while minimizing the impact on the host's memory and timing.

You're way ahead when you have some idea what is likely to fail, derived from testing, industry reports, and case studies. Fault coverage has to be as complete as possible, but we should ensure we have the known failure modes covered. Of course, some failures were missed in testing, resulting in their presence becoming known even in the operational environment.

It is also critically important to know exactly what software has been loaded into the flight computer. What if you have multiple copies, and don't know which one is in orbit. Configuration Control prevents that, right? It has happened.

There is also now a general policy of "test what you fly, fly what you test." You might have included diagnostic code for integration testing, and pull it out before flight. Wrong. Now the code you are going to fly is untested. The tested version include the instrumentation code. Even though it will never be used, it takes up some space, so cache footprints, memory boundary's, and pipeline contents are different.

We also need to carefully consider the failure recovery. Sometimes, we will need the system to reboot itself. That's disruptive, but necessary in some cases. We want to take every possible path before going down that one.

CPU failures are fairly rare, but the flight computer is operating in a hostile environment. There are known failure modes in this environment, that have to be covered. Failures will be transient or hard. Sometimes, hard failures result in a state that is not recoverable. Transient failures, on the other hand, are the hardest to find. We can observe the results, and try to work backward to the root cause. That is where good up-front analysis and data from system test is invaluable. Some architectures, such as the ARM Cortex-R7 have built-in hardware failure detection. That's a good approach, but it leaves many potential failures uncovered.

Here are some potential RHS modules. There is some overlap and duplication in functionality. The impact on system performance should be determined during test. Some of these modules address other areas beyond radiation-damage. Just because the cpu is in a high radiation environment, doesn't mean a spurious interrupt can't occur.

We can tap industry best practices code for system testing. We can also use testing code developed for system POST (power-on-self-test) as an example. POST is accomplished after a reset, but before the system begins to run operational code. It does allowed for checking internal functionality. POST should certainly be included in our repertoire. POST doesn't have specific run time requirements (except the annoyance threshold). A large block of memory can be tested in sections, to avoid adversely affecting system timing.

Developing Flight Software

Developing flight software for a Cubesat doesn't require an

elaborate support system. However, the software is mission critical, and should be developed and tested carefully. After years of effort and lots of money, you don't want to have your Cubesat go dark due to a software issue. Checkout good software engineering practices, and research failure cases.

First, the software should be written with ease of debugging in mind. Documentation should be developed along with the software, and kept updated. A software repository is a good tool. Ideally, the code should be tested by some one other than the developer. Testing is a discipline and a mindset different than development. You know your code will work. You wrote it, right?

When you're writing and integrating the software, define your data structures first, then then implement the algorithms that will implement the desired processing. Use a modular approach, with building blocks that can be tested by themselves, and then integrated together,

Resources are scarce on a Cubesat, so some code may need to be optimized, for time or space. Get it working first, then optimize as required. You may also need to optimize to minimize power consumption.

There is some debate about this practice, but the general approach is "test what you fly, and fly what you test." In other words, leave the instrumentation code in place. If you remove instrumentation code, what you are left with is untested. You have moved code around in memory, affecting cache behavior, and the order of instructions in the pipeline.

OpSys

An *operating system* (OS) is a software program that manages computer hardware and software resources, and provides common services for execution of various application programs. Without an operating system, a user cannot run an application program on their computer, unless the application program is itself self-booting, and has an initiation module, that does the necessary hardware set-up.

For hardware functions such as input, output, and memory allocation, the operating system acts as an intermediary between application programs and the computer hardware, although the application code is usually executed directly by the hardware and will frequently call the OS or be interrupted by it. Operating systems are found on almost any device that contains a computer. The operating system functions need to be addressed by software (or possibly hardware), even if there is no entity that we can point to, called the Operating System. In simple, usually single-task programs, there might not be an operating system per se, but the functionality is still part of the overall software.

An operating system manages computer resources, including:

- Memory.
- I/O.
- Interrupts.
- Tasks/processes/application programs.
- File system
- clock time.

The operating system arbitrates and enforces priorities. If there are not multiple software entities to arbitrate among, the job is simpler. An operating system can be off-the-shelf commercial or open source code, or the application software developer can decide to build his or her own. To avoid unnecessary reinvention of the wheel an available product is usually chosen. Operating systems are usually large and complex pieces of software. This is because they have to be generic in function, as the originator does not know what application space it will be used in. Operating systems for desktop/network/server application are usually not applicable for embedded applications. Mostly they are too large, having many components that will not be needed (such as the human interface), and they do not address the real-time requirements of the embedded domain.

Adapting a commercial or open source operating system to a particular embedded domain can be tricky. Usually, the commercial operating systems need to be used "as-is" and the source code is not available. The software can usually be configured between well-defined limits, but there will be no visibility of the internal workings. For the open source situation, there will be a multitude of source code modules and libraries that can be configured and customized, but the process is complex. The user can also write new modules in this case.

Operating Systems designed for the desktop are not well suited for embedded There were developed under the assumption that whatever memory is required will be available, and real-time operation with hard deadlines is not required.

Real-time operating systems, as opposed to those addressing desktop, tablet, and server applications, emphasize predictability and consistency rather than throughput and low latencies. Determinism is probably the most important feature in a real-time operating system.

A microkernel operating system is ideally suited to embedded systems. It is slimmed down to include only those features needed, with no additional code. Barebones is the term sometimes used. The microkernel handles memory management, threads, and communication between processes. It has device drivers for only those devices present. The operating systems may have to be recompiled when new devices are added. A file system, if required, is run in user space. MINIX, as an example of a streamlined kernel, with about 6,000 lines of code.

For computer systems like the Raspberry Pi, there are enough resources to run an operating system – in fact, it runs Linux. But linux is NOT a real time operating system. It can be patched to operate better in real-time applications, or a custom open source product such as FreeRTOS can be used.

For Arduino-based boards, the architecture is just getting

sophisticated to run an operating system. In many cases, an operating system is not needed. Keep in mind, that some operating system functions still need to be implemented. Setting up the interrupt vectors at initialization is an example. The tasks that the computer has to do might be simple enough that a simple software loop architecture can do the job, perhaps with interrupts.

File Systems

Use of an industry-standard file system will ease the interface to ground based storage and processing. There are several popular file systems, usually defined as part of a specific operating system. A file system provides a way to organized your data, and file systems management services are part of the operating system. The operating systems may support several file formats. A file system organizes data. It presents a data-centric view of a digital storage system.

A file is a container of information, usually stored as a one-dimensional array of bytes. Historically, the file format and the nature of the file system were driven by the mechanism of data storage. On early computer tape units for mainframes, the access mechanism was serial, leading to long access times. With disk and solid-state storage, the access time is vastly improved, as the device is random access – the same access time applies for any data item.

Metadata includes information about the data in a file. This consists of the file name and type, and other parameters such as the size, date and time of creation, the data and time of last access, the owner and read/write/access permissions, when a backup was last made, and other related information.

A directory, like the manila file folder, is a special file that points to ("contains") other files. This allows files to be organized, and implements a hierarchical file system.

There are many file system standards. The Microsoft operating systems support the FAT and NTFS file systems among others. The FAT (File Allocation System) format originated with early support of 8-bit microprocessor systems with MS-DOS. Fat-12 and

FAT-16 had restrictions on the number of files in the root file system, but this has largely been removed with the introduction of FAT-32. File names are restricted to 8 characters, with a 3-character type specifier, the 8.3 format for file names. There are plenty of choices; don't re-invent the wheel.

Onboard interfaces

A bu*s architecture* is used as a short-distance communications pathway between functional elements, such as the cpu and memory. Busses can be serial or parallel. The length of parallel signal lines is severely restricted by bit skew, where all the bits don't necessarily get to a particular point at the same time. This is due in some part by the differing characteristics of the parallel wires or traces implementing the bus. Each path must be treated as a transmission line at the frequencies involved, must have balanced characteristics with all the other lines, and be properly terminated. We'll discuss some common I/O interfaces used in embedded, particularly space systems.

PCI Express

PCI Express is a serial bus that replaced standard pci and the specialized AGP bus. The PCI special Interest group (PCI-SIG) is an industry group of some 900 companies. It is the bus architecture of choice for current desktops, laptops, and servers. It is a point-point system that uses packets used for data. Besides its use on motherboards, it can be extended with cabling.

I^2C

The *Inter-Integrated Circuit* (I^2C) bus is designed for short-range communication between chips on a board. It is a 2-wire interface that is multi-master, and bidirectional. There are 7-bit slave addresses, so 128 unique devices can be addressed from the current master. It was developed by Philips Semiconductor in the 1980's, and is widely used in embedded systems.

SPI/Microwire

The *Serial Peripheral Interface* (SPI) bus is a full-duplex synchronous serial communication system. It is a master/slave architecture. It uses four wires for the serial clock, the master-in/slave-out, the master-out/slave-in, and a slave-select. It is the basis for the *JTAG* (Joint Test Action Group)'s diagnostic interface, and has found application in general I/O device interfacing as well. Microwire is a SPI predecessor, that is half-duplex.

CAN

The *Controller Area Network* (CAN) dates from 1983, and has its origins in industrial control and automation. It was developed by Robert Bosch GmbH in 1986, has been widely used in the automotive industry. It has a message-based protocol, and is a multi-master broadcast serial bus. The theoretical limit for devices on the bus is over 2,000, but a practical limit is about 100. It is a two-wire, half-duplex arrangement. It operates at a conservative 1 mbps, and has error detection and containment features. It is widely used in embedded systems and space applications. It is a proprietary standard.

RS-422/423

These are ANSI and international standards. They use a balanced voltage, or differential scheme. They can be implemented in a multi-drop or point-point architecture. The standards are for the electrical signaling only. RS-423 uses unbalanced signaling at 4 Mbps, over twisted pair. These communication schemes use differential drivers over a 2-wire link. Common ground reduces the effect of external noise and cable effects. Voltage swings can be minimized, (faster transmission and less cross-talk) and less susceptible to voltage differences between the grounds of transmitter and receiver. RS-485 is an enhanced RS-422. There can be 32 drivers and 32 receivers on a bi-directional bus. The line typically terminated at the ends by resistors. Addressing uses a polled master/slave protocol.

Spacewire

Spacewire is IEEE standard 1355. It was developed at the European Space Agency (ESA), and represents a full-duplex, point-to-point route-able protocol. A routable protocol has both a network address and a device address. I can forward packets from on network to another. TCP/IP is a routable protocol. Spacewire operates to 400 megabits per second. Space-rated radiation tolerant parts are available, as are IP cores. A new standard called SpaceFibre is emerging for higher data rates, and routable protocols.

MIL-STD-1553

MIL-STD-1553 is a digital time division multiplexed command/response multiplex avionics bus, used in aircraft and spacecraft, dating from 1973. It uses a coax cable medium, and Manchester bi-phase encoding for code and data transmission. There is a bus controller (BC) and remote terminals (RT's). RT-RT data transmission is allowed, under control for the Bus Controller master. 1553 uses 16-bit words, at a rate of 1 megabit per second. A follow-on standard, 1773, extends the data transmission rate, and uses optical fiber media.

Software bus

The term software bus refers to a mechanism that allows modules or processes to exchange information without worrying about the details of the underlying hardware. It is a virtual bus, with the functionality implemented in software.

Cubesat Space Protocol

This is a network layer protocol, specifically for Cubesats, released in 2010 It features a 32-bit header with both network layer and transport layer data. It is written in the c language, and works with linux and FreeRTOS. The protocol and its implementation is Open source. At the physical layer, the protocol supports CAN bus, I2C, RS-232, TCP/IP, and CCDSDS space link protocol.

Attitude determination and control

To discuss attitude determination and control, we need to delve into Physics, discussing coordinate systems, kinematics, and dynamics.

The attitude of a spacecraft, regardless of the size, can be determined by inertial platforms, and with reference to external bodies such as the Sun, the Earth, the Moon, or the stars. For Cubesats in low Earth orbit, the in-place GPS system can be used. Besides our onboard orbital model, we might need models for the Sun and moon positions, a star map, and a magnetic field map.

With the proscription against using thrusters on Cubesats, the units are confined to passive stabilization such as gravity gradient, internal momentum wheels, which have to be unloaded now and then, or magnetic thrusters.

The gravity field of the Earth is not at all uniform, and this effects satellites in free fall. In addition, the solar wind provides a bias. The drag of the Earth's atmosphere, even at orbital distances, also tends to force the Cubesat to slow down, and eventually re-enter.

Our points of reference include the sun and the Earth. The sun is easily seen (if it is visible form our position – the brightest light in the sky. Of course, it's not much help at "night" when the Earth comes between the Cubesat and the Sun. But, there's good old Earth. It's big, and its warm, compared to space. An "Earth sensor" can scan and see the transitions from warm to cold. For attitude control in the body frame, we'll probably use inertial sensors – MEMS gyros. Every once and a while, we have to adjust the gyros by referencing a known position, like the Sun. For a less exact attitude with respect to the Earth, we can use a 3-axis magnetometer, and a magnetic field model, stored onboard.

Electrical Power

Electrical power is a critical resource. The power system of the spacecraft will consist of batteries, solar cells for recharging, and a charge regulator. In Earth orbit, the spacecraft is constantly moving from full sun to Earth shadow each orbit. Sometimes, the available energy in the batteries must be taken into account when planning operations. Big power users are RF transmission, and onboard computation.

The latest generation of triple junction solar cells achieve up to 30% efficiency in converting light to electrical power. The latest lithium-ion batteries are around 200 watt-hours per kilogram.

A peak power tracker circuit serves as a "transformer" or impedance matcher between the solar arrays and the batteries/electrical loads, adjusting the impedance load the arrays "sees" for optimum transfer of power. It is a dc/dc stepdown converter.

It is also possible to generate electricity with a long, conductive tether, which is just a wire moving in th Earth's magnetic a field. This does, however use kinetic energy from the Cubesat, slowing it and lowering the orbit.

Harness

Harness refers to the wiring interconnect, the power and data backbone between connections. The harness will also include connectors. In the harness, the wires must be the right rating ("gage") and, like anything else, derated. There is usually a series of "break-out boxes" for each connector, to allow access to signals and power, but also to minimize the number of physical connector mate/demate cycles. There should be a "safe-to-mate" procedure that, among other things, will have you verify that power is off before connection. It is a good practice to log the number of connects and disconnects of connector pairs.

EMI/EMC

Electromagnetic Interference, and Electromagnetic Compatibility, are topics that need to be discussed. The Cubesat is launched powered down, so their should be no interference with or from the other payloads or the launch vehicle. Everything radiates. The biggest internal source is the cpu itself. A Cubesat remains powered off for a short while after deployment.

Thermal Management

Most cubesats use passive thermal control. This involves the use of thermal blankets on the Cubesat, made of multi-layer insulation. This is a minimum risk approach, and this technique has been in use for decades. The insulation is multiple (10's) of layers of aluminized mylar with kapton between the layers. Kapton, a Dupont product, has been in use since the 1960's. The blankets are fragile, and easily torn (say, during deployment). Passive thermal control is inexpensive and low risk (high TRL).

Another passive thermal control technique involves paint. Black to absorb heat, white to reflect it. These are standard, high-TRL items, and somewhat expensive, but the Cubesat doesn't have much surface area. Solar cells on the outer surface, on top of thermal blankets, also serve as an insulating layer.

Active thermal control uses power. It might consist of having the spacecraft spin, the bar-b-que maneuver, to equalize heating and cooling (this was used on Apollo lunar missions). Sometimes, active heaters (using electrical power) are needed for sensitive instruments

Telemetry & Command

This section covers the communications between the in-orbit element, and the ground. First, some definitions are in order. "Uplink" is ground to satellite, and "Downlink" is satellite to ground. Uplink usually involves smaller bandwidth, because we are sending commands, or small amounts of data. Downlink can be large in volume, and require significant time and energy. Commands and data are best organized as standard packetized data, and error control mechanisms can be included.

Packets are bundled data, handled identically by the transmission system. Think of them as containers of data, in the same way that standardized containerized freight revolutionized global freight delivery. The standard container is compatible with rail, road, and water transportation. The packet, with its data content moves by radio, or optical fiber, landline, satellite link, and more. Besides the information ("payload"), the packet contains control information such as receiver address, sender address, packet number (for payloads spread across packets), possibly error detection and correction information, etc. In the seven layer network model, packets are data units at level three. The data payload of a packet can be variable length.

Here again, there is advantage to adhering to standards. You could use your own format and protocols, but then you would not be compatible with any one else's equipment. All things considered, don't re-invent the wheel. Use the well-thought-out and well-tested protocols. There is some overhead and perhaps complexity not necessarily needed for a small mission, but the advantages of sticking to a standard format will generally outweigh these.

CCSDS Packets are used on near-Earth and Deep Space communication links. These have more rigorous error detection and correction schemes. The data length is variable, and can be from 7 to 65,542 bytes, which includes the header. Packet sizes are fixed length. The transmission of packets is via data frames, which are also fixed length. The frame contains control information, as well as data.

Cubesat T&C

Most Cubesats are low cost, University-class missions and the Cubesat community needs low cost telemetry and command support. One approach is provided by Satnogs (satnogs.org), which is a low cost, cooperative satellite ground station and network. It uses a modular architecture , with a global management architecture that allows for remote operation of multiple, geographically-dispersed ground stations. It is based on open source hardware and software.

There is a large number of compatible ground stations around the world, operated by schools or individuals. These are all tied together, over the Internet. Each agrees to handle other's telemetry and commanding. An example installation is at MakerFaire in New York. It features a Yagi antenna for 144.8 MHz, and a helical antenna for 437 MHz.

The Satnogs website provides all the information for building the necessary antenna, the ground receiver, and the Internet connection, as well as the software. The tracking system for the antennas is 3-D printable, and driven by stepper motors. The baseline configuration includes the BeagleBone Black or the TP-Link TL-WR703N ($25.) single-board computer. Running Debian Linux or OpenWrt, it supports all ground station functionality (status, tracking, signal receiving and processing) over LAN or WiFi for extreme mobility or remote operation. (https://satnogs.org). This is a project form the Technical University in Athens, Greece, who have their own Cubesat in orbit.

The Global Educational Network for Satellite Operations (Gemso) is a software standard, started at ESA, with a series of ground stations around the world. It was developed for Cubesats, and started in 2007.

There is a Ground Station Server, and a Mission Control Client in the software architecture. Additionally, there is an Authentication Server, to restrict access to registered satellites, and authorized users. The Amateur Radio Community, worldwide, provides the Radio Frequency (RF) equipment and services. Ground stations operate 24x7. The Genso software is written in Java.

Ref:
http://m.esa.int/Education/Global_Educational_Network_for_Satellite_Operations

Onboard command receivers and telemetry transmitters can use common Software Defined Radio techniques. The Raspberry Pi is capable of providing these services, at the 433 MHz level.

NASA provides telemetry and command support for its own Cubesat missions, using its existing Near Earth Network and Space

Network (TDRSS). The agency is planning to support lunar, L1/L2, and Mars missions, which is a challenge due to distance, and the small Cubesat antenna and limited power budget.

Radio Frequency

An Amateur radio operator's license is required from your home country for the Cubesat to include a transmitter, and for the ground station. In the U.S., this is handled by the FCC. Generally, the Cubesat uplink/downlink is around 433 MHz, which can be handled with Software Defined Radio (SDR) code in something like a Raspberry Pi.

Generally, a Cubesat in low Earth Orbit cannot carry a transmitter to talk through the Tracking & Data Relay Satellites at Geosynchronous. We will be transmitting (and receiving) from a ground station at, say 433 MHZ. There are several networks of ground stations. We probably won't get to use NASA or private commercial resources, because they are in heavy use and expensive. This restricts us to transmission only when over ground. (No more Apollo-era tracking ships.).

UHF and VHF off-the-shelf transceivers for Cubesats are available commercially. There are also some S-band units, using patch antennas. Deployable antennas are allowed, and used for the lower frequencies. The higher the frequency, the greater the downlink bandwidth can be. There is also an impact on solar array size, due to greater downlink power.

It is also possible for a Cubesat to use the Globalstar satellite constellation for continuous communication to and from the ground. The radio unit is off-the-shelf. There are 40 satellites in 1,400 km Earth orbit, and 14 ground stations. Data plan rates can be an issue, but start at around $40. At the moment, data is handled in 15 second bundles, in SMS format, or 9,600 bps packets.

Ground Segment

The ground segment for a space mission includes the Control center, the land lines and RF links, the uplink transmitters and downlink receivers, and the antenna system.

This section will discuss the ground-based radio frequency transmitters and receivers for Cubesat operations support.

Ground station – handles the RF part of the uplink and downlink

The Ground segment consists of:

- Antennas, Radio Frequency (RF) gear, communications lines

- Link between the control center and the satellite.

- Data archived at the receiving site, in case of interruption in communication with the control center

Structure

Most cubesat prototypes are built in a printed plastic structure for checking fit. A metal structure is required for flight. Numerous company's offer these for sale, and you are free to fabricate your own. Check the material against the Cubesat spec, and it would not hurt to develop a Finite element model.

Cubesat deployer

Generally, the deployers are compatible with almost any launch vehicle, and a single dispenser can hold three 1U cubesats (or, one 3U). Cubesats take advantage of ride sharing, not only with their fellow Cubesats going to the same orbit, but with the primary payload. The primary payload defines the target orbit, because it is paying the most. If you need a specific orbit for your Cubesat, it will cost time or money.

P-POD

The Poly-Picosatellite Orbital Deployer was a joint project of CalPoly and Stanford. It presents a simple interface to the Cubesat, and handles the details of integration and interface with the launch vehicle. All Cubesats are launched powered-off, and power up (hopefully) shortly after deployment. The standard device holds three, and a double version that can hold six 1U's, or a single 6U six-pack. A multiple payload adapter deploys p-pods. The ejection system uses a pusher plate, and a spring. The exit velocity of the Cubesat is 1.6 meters/second by design.

The p-pod is constructed from 7075-T73 aluminum. The container serves as a Faraday cage, isolating the Cubesats from charged particles or RF interference, and protecting the primary payload from possible RF interference from the Cubesat. It also handles the launch loads, and vibration.

Other options

There are currently no launch vehicle options for just Cubesats. Thus, they ride along as secondary payloads, when a primary mission is going to the right orbit, and has some weight margin.

The University of Tokyo offers T-POD, the Tokyo Picosatellite Orbital Deployer), first flown in 2003. This was developed in cooperation with the University of Toronto. It holds three 1U units. They also offer the CSS, the CUTE Separation System. There is also a German unit, the SPL, or single Picosat Launcher. The Naval Postgraduate School (Monterey, California) for up to 8 Cubesats. It was first used in 2012.

The Nanosat Launch Adapter System, NLAS, is a joint project of NASA-Ames and the DoD. It is designed to handle eight 3U's, or various combinations of other sizes. It provides accommodation for the primary payload as well. It launched its first payloads in 2013.

Safety

Besides the safety of the cubesat payload itself, we should consider safety for you, the builder, the tester, the launch vehicle, the co-payloads, pad personnel, integration and test personnel, and facilities. There is a system engineering approach, and lists of best practices for Safety. Like security, it can't be added later. It is a requirement, and must be addressed at the architecture and design phases.

The Cubesat Operations Control Center

The Cubesat operations Control Center will support development of the Cubesat, which means it needs to be built before the Cubesat itself, or perhaps in parallel. This facilitates an evolving architecture, and will also serve for training of the Cubesat operators, for on-orbit operations.

We start with a document accompanying the Cubesat, that defines th Operational concept. This flows from a high level, what the mission goal s are, to how these goals are achieved. This big picture document will force us to think things through, and will lead to requirements definitions.

It will support code development and debugging and a code archive. Similarly it will support hardware development and testing, and Project documentation.

In the early phase of the build, the Cubesat will exist as a "FlatSat," all the electronics laid out on a table for easy access. The control center, serving as a Test and Integration facility, will provide Debug support hardware and software. This approach allows the control center hardware, software and procedures to be validated along with the flight hardware and software, so the Control Center can be used to support launch and in-flight operations. It will provide command, telemetry, monitoring, and data archive, and may support support onboard science.

In most cases, the engineering-biased control center will have a "quick-look" capability for science (payload) data, but will transfer the relevant data and meta-data to a specialized science data processing facility.

Control center interfaces include, the Internet, via standard infrastructure, the Flatsat via serial or wifi, a Cubesat under test, via serial/USB, a Cubesat in orbit, via RF links, and t o Ops and subsystems personnel, via website, text, email

One particularly interesting Control Center software package is the Open Source COSMOS product from Ball Aerospace. This can was hosted on a standard desktop or laptop machine. Since COSMOS is open source, it can be modified to provide telemetry data from the Cubesat directly to an Apache web server, running on the same host machine. The Telemetry data, once posted on the website, can be accessed by other computers over the web, and by tablets and smart phones.

The modularity and open design of COSMOS greatly enables the project. COSMOS includes 15 modules to send commands; receive, archive, and visualize data; monitor red and yellow limits; and can support automated procedures.

The Control Center function can be implemented totally open source. This includes the COSMOS software running under Ubuntu Linux, and the Apache webserver. Using features of the COSMOS system, formatted and limit-checked telemetry are passed to the web server. This allows the end user terminal to be laptops, tablets, smartphones, or other personal devices.

COSMOS can support more than active satellite missions. In one case I am familiar with the engineering lab was located in an adjacent room. The Cubesats communicated with the control center via wifi. The Flatsats in the lab could be tested from the COSMOS system. Supporting both test and operations allowed for a single architecture that was co-developed with the hardware. The advantage of this approach is that there was not a separate Integration & Test support system and Operations System. When Integration and Test was completed, the Operations Support Software was ready, and validated. This saves considerable time and money. In addition, the system could support multiple Cubesat "targets" simultaneously on the same machine. The number depends solely on bandwidth, memory, and computation cycles available. The solution is scalable, and can be virtualized.

In terms of a lights-out operation, where relevant personnel receive converted data via web access, email, or text message, the control center function has been abstracted. There is still a control center, but you don't need to be there to do your job. It can be operated lights out. A key item to consider is inter-team communication, provided by various corroborative meeting aps. This removes the requirement that team members be co-located. At the same time, routine monitoring of events and trends can be handled by control center software, a virtual system engineer on console 24x7, who doesn't need to sleep or go to the bathroom. This agent software can learn the characteristics of the system, as it ages. We hesitate to use the term artificial intelligence here, but...

Telemetry received by COSMOS is logged as binary, and goes through the Telemetry Extractor process, which produces a text file. It can then be viewed as packets, as extracted telemetry, Engineering units, or graphed. There is also a limit checking process that can be set up on selected telemetry. This involves defining yellow and red limits for each telemetry point.

The link between COSMOS and Apache was implemented by taking the Telemetry Extractor's file and converting it from text to HTM format. This new files were accessible to the Apache web server. The data was put up on the local web, and could be viewed remotely.

COSMOS is implemented in Ruby, an open source, object-oriented language. COSMOS refers to the system it is communicating with as the"target." Thus, we defined the command and telemetry files for the target "Pi." We could support multiple targets with unique identifiers.

We applied increased automation to reduce the manual workload. Routine operations can be handled by the systems itself, with oversight. Automated detection and response to anomalies can be implemented. A wide range of situational awareness tools with visibility across subsystems can be implemented and verified.

Consider the alert system. The easiest implementation is a simple, predefined red-limits, yellow-limits monitoring. As time progresses, the hardware ages, and the limits need to be adjusted.

At the same time, the limits monitor can learn and become smarter, both about pre-set limits, but also about the interaction of multiple sampling points. Alerts can be distributed by pop-up boxes on screens, or test message.

Further additions and improvements can include a secure remote commanding capability, limits-violations text messages, and a "smart" limits checker, that acts as a virtual system engineer on console, deciding when human intervention is needed. This automation of routine tasks allows the control center staff to focus on the exceptions.

Other off-the shelf Control Center software packages include NASA/GSFC's ITOS and Epoch2000 from Kratos Integral Systems. These all are in line with NASA and Industry best practices.

Further functions for the control center include a Cubesat simulator and a software behavioral model for training and validation. Alternately, an hardware engineering model (non-flight) can be used as well. One important thing to keep in mind – uniquely tag the data as "simulated." This is so you know if you're talking to the simulator or the spacecraft.

For the software simulator, it can start as a simple stimulus-response model, and grow to include a dynamics model, thermal model, electrical power model, etc. The simulator should be evolvable.

The Control Center will keep the mission elapsed time, track consumables onboard the satellite, distribute science payload data,. conduct Orbit and visibility analysis, using software such as the STK software package, and do trending, limits check, and sanity check using tools such as MatLab.

Personnel and roles

Within the Control Center, to support on-orbit operations, the following personnel are required:

- Mission Ops Manager (Mom) – in charge. Usually a System engineer.
- Orbit and attitude engineer.
- Thermal engineer.
- Electrical systems engineer. (hardware).
- Onboard data system (software).
- RF Engineer, CMD/TLM – also certified as amateur radio operator, responsible for license adherence.
- Planning and scheduling.
- IT security.

In a small mission, some personnel can provide multiple roles. In really small missions, it could just be you.

Mission Planning and scheduling

The Planning and Scheduling function does not need to be real time, but should always be ahead of wall-clock time. It will result in a detailed, optimized schedule of operations, for a 24-hour period or longer. It may involve complex predictive modeling of the spacecraft and its environment. Once the time-line is verified, it will be mapped into commands and sent to the spacecraft for execution. There are also contingencies for special conditions and anomalies. These are done ahead of when they are needed.

Some items that might have to be factored into the time-line include entrance and exit from the South Atlantic Anomaly (SAA) radiation zone, which might require turning off certain sensitive equipment. There is also the issue of Earth occultation (when the spacecraft is on the opposite side of the Earth from the Sun, and thus has no solar power), and possibly a lunar eclipse, which will also block the Sun.

If we are relying on sensing the Earth's rim to keep pointing to a desired terrestrial target, we must also know when the Sun will blind the horizon sensor. It is also possible that the moon will be partially obscured by the Earth from the spacecraft's point of view, and a horizon sensor would see that as a "bigger" Earth. We need to know when the spacecraft is in line-of-sight with a ground station and when it has no-communication "dark zones."

Engineering support, or housekeeping activities, are accomplished according to schedule, or in response to conditions. An example is momentum unloading. To keep properly oriented, the spacecraft may use momentum wheels. These are spun at high speed to move the much more massive spacecraft in the opposite rotation, slowly. The problem is, there are biases in the gravity field that cause the momentum wheels to become saturated at some point, days, usually. How can we get rid of this momentum, there's nothing to push against? Actually, there is. We can push against the Earth's magnetic field. That requires a map of the field, from the spacecraft's point of view. Momentum wheel unloading can be adjusted accordingly.

Another commodity that has to be tracked is the amount of onboard storage for data. This might fill up, and need to be "dumped" to the ground when a communication channel is available. The spacecraft will need to point its solar arrays for getting the maximum power, its communication antenna to get the best signal, and perhaps movable parts of the science payload.

Onboard status monitoring is common today, but should still be backed up with ground-based monitoring and trending. It is usual to have spare components (4 momentum wheels when we only need three; redundant radios, etc). Spares management and planning for "Plan B"is critical when configuration changes are needed due to degradations and failures. Part of this can be derived from a good Failure Modes and Effects Analysis (FMEA) done during the design and testing process, and kept updated throughout the program.

Anomaly and emergency contingency operations

In a problem scenario onboard the spacecraft, the first line of defense is the onboard computer and its software. It can be considered the first responder. In fact, the ground may not even be aware of the problem for hours. The onboard system has the interfaces, and, ideally, the pre-arranged solution to the problem. If transmitter A fails, turn it off, and turn on B. In the Control center, the operations team has to rely on telemetry (or the lack of it) to diagnose the problem, and come up with a procedure to fix it, and the mission. No pressure. Ideally, an inclusive list of failure scenarios have been postulated, and corrective actions defined. Failing that, we have a hugely expensive, amazingly complex system in a extreme environment to diagnose and fix over a limited bandwidth link. Here, the most senior and knowledgeable operations personnel are called in to the control center. Originally, all fault repairs and workarounds would be determined in the control center, and uplinked to the spacecraft. Now, more capable onboard computers are tasked with the initial part of that job, with the control center as backup. They are at the scene of the problem.

Off-line analysis & trending; performance assessment

One role that can be done in the Control Center's back-room is analysis and trending of the telemetry data. This is not a real-time task, and can be done as a background task. This leads to assessments of the spacecraft subsystems performance, and identifies trends, such as battery degradation and decreased thermal performance. These are usually gradual effects, and don't require up-to-the-moment real-time attention.

NASA GSFC's Integrated Trending and Plotting (ITPS) tool is an example. It implements data retrieval, filtering, and reporting functions. It has a remote web interface, and is pc-based.

Calibration is another engineering task, As the mission progresses, equipment ages, and previously valid calibration curves derived from testing need updating

Data Archiving

Data archiving of all incoming Cubesat telemetry data, and outgoing commands, is done in the control center, using COTS database tools. Off-site data repository's may be used. If the data is important, keep multiple copies in different places.

Spacecraft Simulator

A good software simulator is critical in the Control Center, particularly for initial checkout and for personnel training. The simulator can be developed before or concurrent with the Control Center itself, and used for validation. In operational use, the simulator can be used for anomaly investigation and to develop new scenarios. It can implemented on the same computer architecture that drives the displays and does the calculations in the control center, or it can be a dedicated box.

It is essential that the simulator data be tagged in the header. Don't do what I did once, which was command the simulator, while wondering why the spacecraft was not responding. There's only one thing worse – commanding the spacecraft while viewing simulated data. Design this "feature" out.

A Telemetry and Command Simulator is a simple stimulus-response unit. This is adequate at a low level, but we would like to have a software spacecraft, that models dynamics, electrical power, data flow, and others. This means the simulation also has to include a lot of additional models, such as the Sun, the Earth, the moon, the star field, etc. The simulation can be evolved over time and off-the-shelf models are available for many of these functions.

Modeling

A solar model and an atmospheric model are useful, particularly in calculating satellite lifetime. The sun is the major driver of the Earth's atmosphere, and the residual atmosphere at low Earth orbit affects spacecraft due to drag. In sunlight, the atmosphere boils up, and drag increases. NASA maintains these data from its in-place observation systems.

A thermal model of the spacecraft can be developed, as well as a power/energy/state-of-charge model for the electrical sub-system. Maintaining a thermal model of the spacecraft can lead to useful insight into cooling system performance, and can help to avoid extreme temperatures.

Orbit calculations can be supported in the control center, or done by a support facility. Simple modeling tools such as STK (Satellite Tool Kit) can be used. NASA-GSFC has an Open source tool called ODTBX.

Another useful thing to calculate is the ground track of the orbiting spacecraft. This is useful for coordination with ground stations, and to see a downward looking instrument's footprint on the ground.

A power/energy model is useful to make sure the spacecraft batteries are always staying charged. In some cases, operations must be suspended until the batteries are charged.

Early on-orbit checkout.

Typically, the Control Center is the primary user gateway to the spacecraft. It may generate the data products for the end users of the system. In the engineering case, this is the downlinked spacecraft health and status information. The the spacecraft is carrying one or more science instruments, this data is usually passed along to a science data processing and archive center. There can be a high level of automation for routine operations, like scheduled updates, and more directed operations for anomalies. An example of a routine operation that can easily be automated is consumables tracking.

Multiple Control Centers provide redundancy and geographical diversity. It is possible to have a generic Control Center, that is software configurable for different missions on demand. This depends heavily on flexibility of the configuration, and adherence to standards.

Engineering Data Processing

The data is received at the control center, and the engineering or housekeeping data is processed, but in a database, time tagged, and displayed.

For the Cubesat platform we are concerned about the health and status of various subsystems: Electrical Power, attitude control and pointing, thermal, etc. All data received is archived. It should also be the case that all data is backed up, off-site. It was hard and expensive to get the Cubesat upstairs so don't lose the data. If it's important you need at least two copies. This might be a simple as backing up to a thumb drive every day.

The control center will provide a Quick-look capability, and will run the data against pre-defined yellow (caution) and red (alert) limits. Each subsystem (avionics, power, attitude control, thermal...) has its unique data stripped out and sent to the right cognizant engineer (CogE). Some additional data is required to provide the context – this will be defined by the CogE. You might need attitude information to understand a thermal problem.

The control center will convert the telemetry values from binary words to Engineering units, using calibration curves determined during test by the CogE's. During the mission, the calibration curves will change, so it should be easy to update them. That needs accompanying documentation, so the right cal curves are applied to the right data.

Offline or not in real time, we can access the database and do trending. Is a temperature slowly creeping up? Does electronics box 3 keeping drawing more and more power? Reports can be generated and posted automatically by the system. Data from the test phase should also be available for reference.

Science Data Processing

Generally, science (instrument) data is stripped out in the control center, and sent to a specialized science data processing data. It is common for it to be archived with all other telemetry in the control center, but there will also be a science data archive. Most of the time, quick-look capability is provided.

Data Processing Levels

NASA Earth Data products are processed at various levels from Level 0 to Level 4. Level 0 products are raw data at full instrument resolution. At higher levels, the data are converted into more useful parameters and formats. Instruments may produce data at any of these levels. This is the domain of NASA's Earth Observing System Data and Information System (EOSDIS), a large data processing facility dedicated to Earth Science at GSFC. These are their definitions:

Data Level 0

Reconstructed, unprocessed instrument and payload data at full resolution, with any and all communications artifacts (erg., synchronization frames, communications headers, duplicate data) removed. In most cases, the EOS Data and Operations System (EDOS) provides these data to the data centers as production data sets for processing by the Science Data Processing Segment (SDPS) or by a SIPS to produce higher-level products.

Data Level 1A

This is reconstructed, unprocessed instrument data at full resolution, time-referenced, and annotated with ancillary information, including radiometric and geometric calibration coefficients and geo-referencing parameters (e.g., platform ephemeris) computed and appended but not applied to Level 0 data. This is model output or results from analyses of lower-level data (e.g., variables derived from multiple measurements).

Data Level 1B

This is Level 1A data that have been processed to sensor units (not all instruments have Level 1B source data).

Data Level 3

This has variables mapped on uniform space-time grid scales, usually with some completeness and consistency.

Data Level 4

This is model output or results from analyses of lower-level data (e.g., variables derived from multiple measurements).

Remote Debug, and self-diagnostics

Debugging remote systems in orbit s present unique challenges. One of these is the delay in the communications since the Cubesat might not be in a position to communicate when the problem occurs. Systems should ideally be self-diagnosing, because the cost to "phone home" is high.

What we want to know is,

- What happened?

- What can we do?

- How soon can we do it?

You better have this worked out before hand, with your tool, Failure modes and effects analysis. You are going to need a Cubesat simulator, a flatsat with the same software load as the flight unit. You thought debugging on the Flatsat when you had JTAG and 'scopes. If the system was designed with test software built in, you may get lucky. But this is a time of panic, and whether you get the problem diagnosed and fixed depends on how well you thought it out at implementation time.

NASA System Engineering Process

NASA's system engineering process has been developed over a period of decades, and represents "best practices" in getting systems to orbit (not necessarily just Earth) and having them return valuable data. It is worthwhile to study this process and apply it, even when it seems overkill. Space is non-forgiving, and extreme environment.

Documentation

Documentation is critical in any complex project. This includes architecture and design plans, test plans and results, as-built documentation, failure logs, and, generally, a note of anything that happens. Always have as-flown software listings, and as-built drawings. There should only be one version of this.

TRL

The Technology readiness level (TRL) is a measure of a device's maturity for use. There are different TRL definitions by different agencies (NASA, DoD, ESA, FAA, DOE, etc). TRL are based on a scale from 1 to 9 with 9 being the most mature technology. The use of TRLs enables consistent, uniform, discussions of technical maturity across different types of technology. We will discuss the NASA one here, which was the original definition from the 1980's.

Technology readiness levels in the National Aeronautics and Space Administration (NASA)

1. Basic principles observed and reported.
This is the lowest "level" of technology maturation. At this level, scientific research begins to be translated into applied research and development.

2. Technology concept and/or application formulated.
Once basic physical principles are observed, then at the next level of maturation, practical applications of those characteristics can be 'invented' or identified. At this level, the application is still speculative: there is not experimental proof or detailed analysis to support the conjecture.

3. Analytical and experimental critical function and/or

characteristic proof of concept.

At this step in the maturation process, active research and development (R&D) is initiated. This must include both analytical studies to set the technology into an appropriate context and laboratory-based studies to physically validate that the analytical predictions are correct. These studies and experiments should constitute "proof-of-concept" validation of the applications/concepts formulated at TRL 2.

4. Component and/or breadboard validation in laboratory environment.

Following successful "proof-of-concept" work, basic technological elements must be integrated to establish that the "pieces" will work together to achieve concept-enabling levels of performance for a component and/or breadboard. This validation must be devised to support the concept that was formulated earlier, and should also be consistent with the requirements of potential system applications. The validation is "low-fidelity" compared to the eventual system: it could be composed of ad hoc discrete components in a laboratory

TRL's can be applied to hardware or software, components, boxes, subsystems, or systems. Ultimately, we want the TRL level for the entire systems to be consistent with our flight requirements. Some components may have higher levels than needed.

5. Component and/or breadboard validation in relevant environment.

At this level, the fidelity of the component and/or breadboard being tested has to increase significantly. The basic technological elements must be integrated with reasonably realistic supporting elements so that the total applications (component-level, sub-system level, or system-level) can be tested in a 'simulated' or somewhat realistic environment.

6. System/subsystem model or prototype demonstration in a

relevant environment (ground or space).

A major step in the level of fidelity of the technology demonstration follows the completion of TRL 5. At TRL 6, a representative model or prototype system or system - which would go well beyond ad hoc, 'patch-cord' or discrete component level breadboarding - would be tested in a relevant environment. At this level, if the only 'relevant environment' is the environment of space, then the model/prototype must be demonstrated in space.

7. System prototype demonstration in a space environment.

TRL 7 is a significant step beyond TRL 6, requiring an actual system prototype demonstration in a space environment. The prototype should be near or at the scale of the planned operational system and the demonstration must take place in space.

The TRL assessment allows us to consider the readiness and risk of our technology elements, and of the system.

The T&C handbook

The Telemetry & Command Handbook is a crucial document. It contains and defines each command, and each telemetry point for the uplink and downlink. It is now commonly a database. Compiling the T&C handbook begins early in the project, and continues to be updated during flight. It must be a configuration-controlled document. Now it is common to keep the Handbook in electronic form, under configuration control.

Configuration control

The hardware and software configuration of the Cubesat must be documented carefully and completely. Changes can't be arbitrarily made, and not documented There needs to be one place you can go to that contains all the details. At a failure investigation for a Space mission (we won't mention names) the review board requested copies of the flight software. They were given two copies, either of which could be onboard.

Faults

This section discusses faults, how to detect, analyze, contain, and control them.

Engineering Tools

Various system engineering tools are available to use both before and after "incidents." Ideally, we review the systems before hand with respect to failure and safety, and factor these issues into the implementation plan. Many factors marginalize this approach, including management focus, and impact on systems cost and schedule.

After the fact, we have the Root Cause analysis method, so we can determine what exactly failed, and how this particular issue can be addressed and mitigated. In many cases, this process uncovers other latent issues that also need to be addressed. These need to be documented as case studies for the use of future projects.

Root Cause Analysis

Root Cause Analysis refers to an engineering process to identify and categorize the causes of events, and to identify the primal cause. It is a useful tool for determining why a disaster happened. It is used to define the what, how, and why (and sometimes, who)? Its value is that it will lead to a definition of corrective measures that can be applied in the future.

By definition, root causes are underlying, identifiable, and controllable. The RCA process includes a data collection phase (forensics), a cause charting, the root cause identification, recommendations, and implementation of the solution to avoid repeating the error. In many cases, the RCA will uncover other failure causes that were overlooked. There are software tools available to assist in the RCA process.

Keep in mind, your solution should not introduce additional problems.

FMEA

The failure modes and effects analysis is an engineering tool that is applied during the design and testing process of a system. In this approach, we postulate failure modes, and analyze their impact on the system performance. The possible failure modes are examined to confirm their validity. Then, the possible failures are prioritized by severity and consequences. The goal is to identify and eliminate failures in the order of decreasing severity.

The FMEA approach can actually start at the Project conceptual phase, and continue throughout the project life-cycle. It can (and should) be applied to modifications to existing projects. The origins of the FMEA approach were during World War-II, by the U. S. Military. After the war, the approach was adopted by the aviation (aerospace) and automotive industries.

The FMEA analysis requires a cross-functional team, consisting, as applicable of hardware and software engineers, manufacturing, Quality Assurance, test engineers, reliability engineers, parts, and, ideally, the customer.

The process involves identifying the scope of the project, defining the boundaries and the desired level of detail. Then, the system (or project) functions are identified. Each function is analyzed to identify how it could fail. For each of these failure cases, the consequences are noted. These range from no effects to catastrophic. Formally, the consequences are rated on a scale of 1 to 10, with 1 being insignificant to 10, catastrophic. The root cause is then determined for each consequence, starting with the 10's. Software tools are available to support this analysis process.

Once the causes are determined, the controls are defined. Controls prevent the cause from happening, reduce the probability of happening, or detect the failure in time for correction to be applied. For each control, then, a detection probability rating is calculated (or estimated), again on a scale of 1-10. Here, 1 indicates that control is certain, and 10 indicates that the solution will not work. By definition, critical characteristics of the system have a severity of 9 or greater, and have an occurrence and detection rating of greater than 3.

A Risk Priority Number (RPN) is calculated, which is severity times occurrence time detection (ratings). This measure is used to rank failure modes in the order in which they are to be addressed.
Of course, some of these rankings are not measurable, but the result of good engineering guesses
From an FMEA, you can develop contingency plans, adjust to the identified failure scenarios. It is always good to have a Plan B. Also C, D, E......

Fault Tolerant Design

In this design approach, a system is designed to continue to operate properly in the event of one or more failures. It is sometimes referred to as graceful degradation. There is, of course, a limit to the number of faults or failures than can be handled, and the faults or failures may not be independent. Sometimes, the system will be designed to degrade, but not fail, as a result of the fault. Fault recovery in a fault-tolerate design is either roll forward, or roll back. Roll back refers to returning the system state to a previous check-pointed state. Roll forward corrects the current system state to allow continuation.

Redundancy

Redundancy refers to the technique of having multiple copies of critical components. Belt and suspenders; two independent ways to accomplish the same results. Either can fail without affecting the other. This can refer to hardware or software. This increases the reliability of the system. Redundant units can be deployed in parallel, such as extra structural members, where each single unit can handle the load. This provides what is referred to as a margin of safety.

In certain systems that are responsible for safety-critical tasks, we might triplicate the critical portion, which, reduces the probability of system failure to small, acceptable, levels. This approach is found in aircraft controls, nuclear power plant controls, and many more, safety-critical systems.

Of course, if there is a common error in the three units, we have not increased our reliability. This situation is referred to as a common mode or single point error. Another problem is in the voting logic, that makes the decision that an error has been made, and switches controllers. At least one satellite launch failed because the voting logic made the wrong choice. Redundancy carries penalties in size, weight, power, cost, and testing complexity.

Fault isolation allows the system to operate around the failed component, using backup or alternative modules. Fault containment strives to isolate the fault, and prevent propagation of the failure.

One principle of fault tolerant design is replication, with multiple copies of critical systems. Of course, this approach is susceptible to common mode errors. A more vigorous approach is Diversity, where the same task may be accomplished with different implementations. This was the approach chosen for the Shuttle's computers. Generally, a fault detection systems needs to be a separate, independent entity. It's probably of error will be smaller than the main system, because it is simpler. But, it must be closely examined for common mode faults, such as a shared power supply.

Systems can be designed to be fail-safe, fail-soft, or can be "melt-before-fail." The more fault tolerant that is built into a system, the more it will cost, and the more difficult it will be to test. It is important not to increase the complexity to the point where the system is not testable, and is "designed to fail."

Fault Tree

A fault tree is a graphical representation of faults and their causes. It provides a top-down deductive analysis for a system. There are software tools to facilitate the construction of the tree, which just allows you to visualize binary decision points. It must be complete (full fault coverage) and correct.

Fault Tolerance

Fault tolerance refers to the feature of a system that allows for certain faults or certain sequences of faults to not affect operation or safety. The system might be said to be capable of graceful degradation. Obviously, there is a limit to how many faults the system can survive, and many faults cause subsequence ripple-effects. Loss of attitude control cause shortage power, which causes communication to be lost...

A defective design can be identified and corrected before it leads to an accident thanks to quality assurance and analysis of flight parameters during testing and operation of any space hardware. This is where complacency comes into play. Failures involving complex systems are always preceded by so-called accident precursors, which take the form of parameters out of tolerance. People responsible for those systems become accustomed to the idea that nothing bad will ever happen because nothing bad has happened yet.

Fault Containment

Fault Containment means we might have a fault, but it can be contained or isolated locally. This minimize the impact of the fault, and keep it from getting worse. Opportunities for fault containment are in the design phase, after a good FMEA has been done. Then, the systems can be analyzed with a goal of minimizing subsequent faults and failures.

Mitigation

Fault mitigation means you have designed the system with what we might call reflex actions in response to a detected fault, and healing actions, that offset the failure. This can't be done across all faults, but an evaluation of the system with various what-if scenarios, may allow for automatic responses to faults.

BIST

Built-in self-test is part of the design-for-testability philosophy. It is applicable at the box, board, or chip level. It defines the inclusion of additional circuitry or code specifically for testing purposes. It may include software components, or diagnostic cores for FPGA's. For example, when a standard pc system is reset, the initial code, in the BIOS, performs a series of functional tests on the hardware of the board hardware. This is generally referred to as POST – Power-On-Self-Test. The technique of BIST was first used operationally on the Minuteman missile.

Integration and Test

First and foremost, a Cubesat is a satellite. You can cut corners on your payload, if you're willing to take risk.

The engineering model of a spacecraft data system is generally referred to as the "FlatSat." It is used for integration and test. Early in the program, the Flatsat would consist of non-flight hardware. It is organized to fit on a table, with easy access to connections, functional boxes, and test points. As the project progresses, the data system will be built up of flight-like or flight boxes, and more care must be given to handling. Internal test points may not be easily accessed at this point in the program.

There is a major advantage to testing the flight system using software that will evolve into the operational environment. Previously, special test software was used, with scripting languages that facilitated testing. These are generally know as STOL – System Test Oriented Languages. These define sequences of command and expected response, with decision points. These carry forward into operational sequences for flight.

JTAG support

Joint Test Action Group (JTAG) is the name for the IEEE-1149.1 standard for a test access point and a boundary scan architecture for integrated circuit level debug. The JTAG effort began in 1985 as a test and fault isolation methodology for board level products.

It is particularly valuable for embedded systems, with limited human interfaces for visibility. It is used in cpu-based systems, FPGA's, and SoC architectures. With the proper application software, the JTAG can access and control test instrumentation included within the chip. JTAG can also be used to load data into internal flash memory. JTAG is used a portal to the chips built-in self test (BIST).

JTAG uses a 4-wire interface (data in, data out, clock, mode select), sometimes with a 5th line, test reset. The data transfer mode is serial, using a short cable. The host side for the JTAG system can be connected via USB or even Ethernet. There are numerous commercial JTAG tool vendors providing multi-platform support, and Open Source tools also exist. Almost all modern embedded architectures provide JTAG support. A 2-wire alternative is Serial Wire Debug, that has the JTAG protocol implemented,.

Security

Has your Cubesat project been hacked? Are you sure? Security applies to the control center, the users, and the embedded controllers onboard the Cubesat.

There are a lot of bored and/or malicious computer experts out there, ranging from State-sponsored to idle teenagers at an Internet Cafe. They all want to play with your Cubesat. Just like anything with a computer, we can have hacking, virus and malware insertion, theft, spoofing, disruption, denial of service, and your Cubesat or control center can be used as a launch point for denial of service attacks against other systems. This has happened to traffic light controllers, ATM's, elevators, trains, planes, and automobiles, and implanted medical devices.

Don't ask if your systems is going to be attacked. Assume it is, and prevent it by Design.

All systems have aspects of security. Some of these issues are addressed by existing protocols and standards for access and communications security. Security may also imply system stability and availability. Standard security measures such as security reviews and audits, threat analyses, target and threat assessments, countermeasures deployment, and extensive testing apply..

Addressing security involves:

- Use of industry standards and best practices
- security audits
- threat analysis
- target assessment
- countermeasures
- testing, testing, testing

A security assessment of a system involves threat analysis, target assessment, risk assessment, countermeasures assessment, and testing. This is above and beyond basic system functionality.

The completed functional system may need additional security features, such as intrusion detection, data encryption, and perhaps a self-destruct capability. Is that self-destruct capability secure, so not just anyone can activate it? All of these additional features use time, space, and other resources that are usually scarce in embedded systems.

Virus and malware attacks on desktops and servers are common, and an entire industry related to detection, prevention, and correction has been spawned. These issues are not as well addressed in the embedded world. Attacks on new technology such as cell phones, tablets, and GPS systems are emerging. Not all of the threats come from individuals. Some are large government-funded efforts or commercial entities seeking proprietary information or market position. Security breaches can be inspired by ideology, money, or fame considerations. The *CERT* (Computer Emergency Response Team) organization at Carnegie Mellon University, and the *SANS* Institute (SysAdmin, Audit, Networking, and Security) track security incidents.

Techniques such as hard checksums and embedded serial numbers are one approach to device protection. Access to the system needs to be controlled. If unused ports exist, the corresponding device drivers should be disabled, or not included. Mechanisms built into the cpu hardware can provide protection of system resources such as memory.

Security has to be designed in from the very beginning; it can't just be added on. Memorize this. There will be a quiz.

Even the most innocuous embedded platform can be used as a springboard to penetrate other systems. It is essential to consider security of all embedded systems, be aware of industry best practices and lessons learned, and use professional help in this specialized area.

The Control Center has issues of security, both operational and data. First, it needs to be a controlled access facility. Only authorized personnel should be in the MCC. But don't forget virtual users. Can the control center computers be hacked into? What ports and backdoors exist in the implementation? Best practices from the Computer/Network Security Industry can be applied.

The Control Center must quickly act quickly to identify and react to cyberattacts. These might be phishing expeditions to steal data, malicious attacks to gain control of space assets, or denial of service attacks. A good penetration-testing of the facility is called for. There should be a permanent Security Officer for data, with the responsibility for data and operations.

Issucs:

- access control
- system stability
- intrusion detection
- data encryption
- time, space, other resources scarce, though

Case Studies of Cubesat Missions

They have been hundreds of Cubesat missions, of which, statistically, half worked. Here is a mention of just a couple of missions.

Brazil's Garatea-L

All over the world, any nation can become spacefaring with a reasonable cost. This ambitious project, to be launched in 2020, is an example. It will orbit the moon, and examine the effects of that environment on different life forms. The project is bing done in cooperation with the UK Space Agency and ESA. Several other Cubesats will tag along for the ride. The Brazilian mission will provide the communications back to Earth for all the associated missions. The launch would be carried out by two British companies and in partnership with the European Space Agency (ESA) and the UK Space Agency, which on the same flight would send the Pathfinder, the first deep space mission of a commercial character.

It is a joint effort among top universities: he National Institute of Space Studies (INPE), the Technological Institute of Aeronautics of USP, the National Laboratory of Synchrotron Light and the Institute of Technology of the Pontifical Catholic University of Rio Grande do Sul, with the University of Sao Paulo in the lead.

Garatea, in the native Tupi-Guarani language means "looking for lives."

Brazil's Tancredo-1

This interesting STEM project by middle school students was sent to the Space Station at the end of 2016, and deployed into space from the Japanese module. It was built from a kit from IOS, in California. It has the support of the Brazilian Space Agency, The National Institute for Space Research, and Unesco. It features a pre-recorded message from one of the school team members, that will be broadcast from orbit.

ZACUBE-1

From the Cape Peninsula University of Technology in South Africa is Africa's first Cubesat. It was built as a project of the South African National Space Agency, with assistance from the French South African Institute of Technology. I was launched on a Russian vehicle in 2013, and is collecting data on space weather. The project has resulted not only in on-orbit success, but 22 Mater's degrees, 10 conference papers, and 3 journal papers. The project also spun off the African Space Innovation Center, with a Research Chair.

NASA Involvement with Cubesats

NASA has been exploring the usage of "Smallsats" for some time, to reduce mission costs and provide rapid development and deployment. When Cubesats came along, it didn't take long for NASA to embrace the technology.

NASA GSFC says, "Current technology trends indicate a shift in satellite architectures from large, single-satellite missions to small, distributed spacecraft missions. At the center of this shift is the SmallSat/CubeSat architecture."

At NASA and many National Labs, Cubesats have been a game-changer. The cost to develop, build, and test a concept or technology has gone down by orders of magnitude. This precursor technology has not only gone down in price, but the implementation process has been accelerated..

A recent NASA/GSFC Cubesat project, Dellingr, is set for launch as this book is being prepared. This will be a 6U (12" x 8" x 4") size. It was a one-year project to design, develop, test, and integrate the unit. It will be heading to the International Space Station. It is a Heliophysics payload, carrying an ion/neutral mass spectrometer. The design will be made available as Open Source after the mission is kicked off.

Another project was the NSF-funded Firefly mission, launched in November of 2013, and now returning good data on terrestrial Gamma ray flashes, These are interesting phenomena, involving high energy electrons generated by thunderstorms. Firefly uses a Pumpkin flight Motherboard for avionics, based on the Texas Instruments MSP430 chip. That unit is a 16-bit RISC microcontroller architecture, The unit is ultra-low power, and mixed signal, supporting analog. It includes a real-time clock, and non-volatile FRAM memory.

Cubesats provide a relatively Low cost alternative for proof of concept, and TRL advancement (explained below). We're talking $1 million, not $$100 million. We take advantage of the modularity and standardization of hardware and software. We have, essentially, *Plug-and-play* satellite buses, provided by an evolving infrastructure of parts suppliers.

NASA's Educational Launch of Nanosatellites (ELaNa) program initiative to get worthy educational and non-profit organization's projects to Orbit.

An interesting NASA/NSF Cubesat called Firefly provided new information on strange space phenomena. It studied Terrestrial Gamma Ray Flashes from violent thunderstorms. It's all in the point of view – Firefly looks down into the storms, and can view the gamma ray flashes, which can't be seen from the ground. Evidently, violent thunderstorms are Nature's particle accelerators

Riding along on the Taurus launch Vehicle with NASA's Glory mission were three Cubesats. Explorer-1 Prime for the Montana State University, the KySat-1 from the Kentucky Space Consortium, and Hermes from University of Colorado. This was the first ElaNa launch, and there have been numerous ones since.

Reference: https://www.nasa.gov/feature/elana-cubesat-launches

JPL, whose interest lies beyond Earth orbit, has worked on more that 14 Cubesat missions. PhoneSat-5 was an early NASA-Ames mission, built around a Nexus cell phone.

Reference: http://www.jpl.nasa.gov/cubesat/missions/

Cubesats on ISS

The NanoRacks Cubesat Deployer by Nanoracks, LLC, is the interface between Cubesats and the International Space Station. It provides mechanical and electrical isolation. The NanoRacks locker is in place in the ISS. Each tray of the locker holds 16 1U Cubesats. More than 200 Cubesats have gone to the ISS.

The commercial NanoRacks platform is a research facility, providing power and data services to the cubesats. The platform itself is 43 by 23 by 50 centimeters. It is used within the pressurized volume of the Station. Each platform can hold 16 Cubesats. The platform is installed in EXPRESS rack inserts, which are ISS standard facilities. The EXPRESS racks can handle payloads other than Cubesats in Nanoracks. A rack has an associated laptop computer to supply data services. Data from the Cubesats in the rack is telemetered to the Huntsville Operations Support Center, via TDRSS. The specific EXPRESS rack for Cubesats is in the Japanese Module. Cubesats can also be deployed outside the station, using an airlock. The external remote manipulator system is used to complete deployment,

They are delivered by the logistics carrier along with food, clothes, and toilet paper. They may also be put on the unmanned logistics carrier which reenters and burns, along with trash and broken equipment. There is the option to return a few Cubesats with one of the Soyuz crew exchange vehicles.

A very interesting approach is MakerSat, which is a Cubesat designed for in-space assembly. At the moment, that means on the ISS. The advantage of just sending up the design files and material, and printing the structure "upstairs" is that the structure does not have to go through the harsh launch environment. This means it can be smaller and lighter. The design files are open source. MakerSat has a 1U frame design. It is easy to assemble (which is good in the zero-g environment), and does not use bolts, screws, or other fasteners, which are easy to lose track of. There are no tools required for assembly.

Lunar Cubesats

Venturing out from Earth, out first destination is the moon. NASA's SIMPLEx mission (Small Innovative Missions for Planetary exploration) has 13 Cubesats lined up for a 2018 launch on an Orion vehicle. This will spend three weeks in space, including 6 days orbiting the moon. Cubesat missions will include the Lunar Flashlight, to look for water ice; the Near-Earth Asteroid Scout (with a solar sail); the BioSentinal, SkyFire, from Lockheed Martin; Lunar Ice Cube; CUSP, Cubesat for Solar Particles, and Lunar Polar Hydrogen Mapper. More will be selected closer to launch time.

Brazil's Garatea-L project, previously discussed, is also targeting the moon.

Marco Project

Mars Cube One (MarCO) is the first interplanetary cubesat mission, headed by JPL. It involves sending two 6-U Cubesats to Mars, along with the Insight Rover. The cubesats will separate at Earth orbit and proceed on their own. The mission was to be launched in March, 2016, when Mars was 1.07 AU distant, and arrive in September of 2016. The launch was postponed, however, due to a vacuum leak in the prime instrument. The mission is rescheduled for 2018, due to a test failure on the main spacecraft.

The Cubesats will serve as a real-time communications relay with Earth during the critical descent and landing phase of the rover. The Rover talks to the Cubesat relays over an 8kbps UHF link, and the Cubesats relay this to Earth over an 8kbps X-band link to the DSN. The Cubesat's X-band antenna is a large flat panel.

The Cubesats are stabilized with reaction wheels, and have propulsion systems to unload the wheels, and adjust their orbital position.

Author's picosat

Thinking that Cubesats are bloated and over-sized, the author prototyped a picosat, using components from TinyCircuits of Akron, Ohio. It is a 3.5 cm cube. The flight computer stack is an Arduino architecture using the Atmega328P, with 32k of flash, 2k of ram, 14 Digital I/O, and 6 Analog I/O. The unique board design has stacking connectors. These is a 433 MHz radio board, a GPS board, a microSD card board (using a 16 Gbyte card), a 9-axis inertial measurement unit with a 3 axis accelerometer, a 3-axis angular rate sensor, and a 3-axis magnetic field sensor. There is a real-time clock, and a 270 mAH rechargeable lithium Polymer battery. Now, where did I put that?

Special Cases – Interplanetary Cubesats

At this time, there are no functional Cubesats outside of the Earth orbit. That changed soon with missions to the moon. In addition, the Marco Mission to Mars, to be launched in 2017, has a pair of tag-along Cubesats with the primary payload. But our experience outside of low Earth orbit is lacking. We have visited all of the planets and some of the moons with large, purpose-built spacecraft.

Up to this point, the application of Cubesats for interplanetary exploration has been approached by building bigger, more robust Cubesats. Here, I will suggest an alternate approach – Launch a mothership loaded with standard Cubesats to a destination of interest.

As we get farther from Earth, the Cubesat's small antennas, and relatively low power, means we have to get clever with communications. JPL's approach is to use laser communications. There will be a limited bandwidth. This happened with the Horizon's spacecraft at Pluto – It will take more than 16 months to transmit all the data back.

At the moment, There is a communications relay satellite in Mars orbit. This is for the Mars rovers on the surface. We can postulate the mothership can be placed into orbit around the target, and provide this service for the Cubesats. JPL is also exploring onboard processing of the data, to a point. This involves, then, a computation-communication trade. Outward, away from Earth, power from the Sun is problematic. When Mars and Earth are on opposite sides of the Sun, communication is not possible. There is a Communications blackout. This is true for all of the planets. This can span a series of days or weeks.

The other problem is the time to get there. The recent Juno mission to Jupiter took 5 years to get to Jupiter. Less to Mars, more for the outer planets. During this time, the spacecraft is exposed to the dangers of space, including galactic cosmic rays. Upon arrival at the target, the systems have to work. We might keep the electronics asleep, but the mechanical systems, starting with the launcher (P-PoD), deployable antennas and arrays need to function. There is a phenomena in the vacuum where similar metals will cold-weld themselves together. It's a different ballgame outside of the Earth-Moon system. Away from the home planet, the restriction on expulsive engine systems can be relaxed. We might have a tag-along as with the Marco mission to Mars, or we may have a large swarm of Cubesats in a Mothership.

Constellations

Constellations are groups of satellites operating together to observe a single target A constellation allows you to do simultaneous observations from multiple locations. The elements of a constellation can be homogeneous or not. With Cubesats, we would have multiple co-operating units. There can be distributed control, or central control.

NASA says, " A Constellation is a space mission that, beginning with its inception, is composed of two or more spacecraft that are placed into specific orbit(s) for the purpose of serving a common objective (e.g., Iridium)"

An example is their Distributed Spacecraft Mission being defined at JPL to allow "formation flying" of multiple spacecraft. Another point of view is the "fractionalized spacecraft", where the spacecraft functionality is distributed across multiple units. Critical to this is a intra-communications mechanism. The Constellation may use a mesh or lattice architecture. The members of this organization can be launched together, or separately. One thing for sure, each unit needs a unique identifier.

These units can be statically or dynamically allocated. We might have a fixed plan for location and function, or it might be ad hoc, responding to conditions as they are encountered.

For Cubesats, we might need a "mothership" that takes the members to their destination, then sticks around to provide support. This approach will be discussed in a section on the Strawman multi-Cubesat mission to Jupiter, later in the book.

Constellations add complexity to the mission. Complexity has two major components, number of units, and number of interactions,

Trains

Trains of satellites refer to multiple units that are generally in the same orbit track, and are spaced along the track. This allows for simultaneous imaging areas, as well as continuous observation of selected areas. It is a co-ordinated group of observation satellites. NASA uses this approach successfully for Earth Science and Weather satellites in polar, sun-synchronous orbits. A train of 5 weather satellites passes over the same spot at the same time every day. The satellites are all different, but provide useful information on atmospheric conditions, and ground condition. Trains of Cubesats could be employed in this manner.

Clusters

In computing, a cluster means a group of loosely coupled elements, working together on the same problem. If the cluster were more tightly coupled, and self-directed, we'd have a swarm. As it is, we would have a group of individuals that could be considered a single entity. Generally, members of a cluster have the same hardware and software configuration. One issue in clustering is the degree of coupling between elements. No coupling means we have a mob. A lot of coupling and we might have a swarm. In a cluster, management of the cluster can be centralized in a "boss" or can be distributed.

Swarms

This section describes a different approach: collections of smaller co-operating systems that can combine their efforts and work as ad-hoc teams on problems of interest. Cubesats can be organized in Swarms.

This is based on the collective or parallel behavior of homogeneous systems. This covers collective behavior, modeled on biological systems. Examples in nature include migrating birds, schooling fish, and herding sheep. A collective behavior emerges form interactions between members of the swarm, and the environment.

A driver in the space environment is the exploration of the asteroids, numbering in the thousands. Although there are fewer than 10 planets, and less than 200 moons, there are millions of asteroids, mostly in the inner solar system. The main asteroid belt is between Mars and Jupiter. Each may be unique, and some may provide needed raw materials for Earth's use. There are three main classifications: carbon-rich, stony, and metallic.

The physical composition of asteroids is varied and poorly understood. Ceres appears to be composed of a rocky core covered by an icy mantle, whereas Vesta may have a nickel-iron core. Hygiea appears to have a uniformly primitive composition of carbonaceous chondrite. Many of the smaller asteroids are piles of rubble held together loosely by gravity. Some have moons themselves, or are co-orbiting binary asteroids. The bottom line is, asteroids are diverse.

It has been suggested that near-Earthasteroids might be used as a source of materials that may be rare or exhausted on earth (asteroid mining) or materials for constructing space habitats or as refueling stations for missions. Materials that are heavy and expensive to launch from earth may someday be mined from asteroids and used for space manufacturing. Valuable materials such as platinum may be returned to Earth for a profit.

Exploring the asteroids requires a diverse and agile system. Thus, a swarm of robotic spacecraft with different capabilities might be used, combining into Teams of Convenience to address situations and issues discovered in situ.

In Swarm robots, the key issues are communication between units, and cooperative behavior. The capability of individual units nodes not much matter; it is the strength in numbers. Ants and other social insects such as termites, wasps, and bees, are models for robot swarm behavior. Self-organizing behavior emerges from decentralized systems that interact with members of the group, and the environment. Swarm intelligence is an emerging field, and swarm robotics is in its infancy.

For a constellation of Cubesats, the Swarm behavior of peer units could be implemented.

Case study – Pinesat

This section will discuss a Cubesat-based alternative trade-study, based on the recent Juno mission to Jupiter. For the baseline, we took the Juno's size and weight, and developed a unique CubeSat carrier vehicle "mothership" which was capable of getting 333 3-U cubesats to Jupiter. These would be dispensed from the carrier once it achieved Jovian orbit, and could be organized in clusters to observe and report on Jupiter's atmosphere, magnetic field, and ring system. The paper project was named Pinesat, due to the appearance of the dispenser/mothership.

The parameters of the Juno mission were used to bound the problem, and examine the feasibility of replacing one large exploration spacecraft with a swarm of smaller ones.

Jupiter's Magnetic field is 20,000 times that of Earth. This would allow for the use of a conductive tether to generate electricity.

One advantage of the carrier is, like the Shuttle, payloads can be tested before deployment from the carrier. Known bad units can be discarded into Jupiter's atmosphere. The carrier is designed to be modular and adaptable. It is scalable to 100's or 1,000's of Cubesats.

The Pinesat mechanical design is straightforward. The name comes from the fact that the dispenser resembles a pine tree. The Pinesat dispenser has a central hexagonal tube, with the propulsion and electrical power section at the launch vehicle interface end. The avionics and data storage are located in the nose of the vehicle while p-pod's are distributed radially along the central tube. This allows for longitudinal deployment. We postulated having 333 p-pod class dispensers, each with a 3-U cubesat inside.

The Pinesat will keep a database of Electronic Data Sheets of all the Cubesats. This includes state-of-charge, operational status, and instrument complement. This can be updated by a query request from the dispenser's main computer.

Unlike Earth Cubesat missions, the Cubesats going to Jupiter can have their own propulsion. The big limiting factor for them is electrical power. They can't carry solar arrays large enough to make sense. They will be dispersed from the carrier fully charged, and operate as long as they can. The electronics and software will be optimized to minimize power usage.

The Cubesats will be 3U, envisioned to use a Raspberry Pi-based flight computer, running GSFC's Core Flight System/Core Flight Software.

The mothership/dispenser will have a bi-propellant engine for orbit and cruise adjustments, and a monopropellant system for attitude control and reaction wheel momentum unloading, like Juno

Pinesat Avionics

The Pinesat dispenser will have dual redundant, rad-hard flight computers such as the RAD-750's. Those were used on Juno. They have 256 megabytes of flash, 128 megabytes of DRAM, and operate at 200 MHz. It will have sufficient storage for the database of Cubesats. It will also host an onboard networks for communications with the Cubesats when they are onboard, and via radio when they have been deployed. The dispenser vehicle hosts the communications links with Earth. The mothership is the communications relay for the Cubesat swarm's science data. It will serve as a "store-and-forward" node, using an x-band transceiver. A laser could also be used.

Ops concept

The Mothership transports the Cubesats to Jupiter unpowered. Every day or week (tbd), units are powered on, one at a time, and checked for functionality. The onboard database is updated as required. The results are sent back to the control center on Earth.

At Jupiter, the Mothership uses its main engine to enter orbit outside of the ring system. It then orients itself in a gravity-gradient attitude, with the solar panels oriented to the Sun. Juno is a spinning spacecraft.

After another system check of the itself and the Cubesats, the Mothership deploys a series of Cubesat scouts on a reconnaissance mission, to seek out areas of interest. The Mothership deploys Cubesats with broad spectral sensing to the areas of interest. Based on their findings, the mothership will deploy Cubesats with specific instrumentation to the area of interest. (For example, an advanced thermal imager to an area of thermal activity). The Cubesats are released in the order of necessity. The Cubesats will be able to adjust their attitude with torquer bars to push against the large Jovian magnetic field. We can also include the idea of Cubesat "suicide mission, where the Cubesat plunges into the ring system, or Jupiter's upper atmosphere, and returns data until it is rendered non-functional.

The Cubesats will:

- Conduct radio occultation experiments to better categorize the distribution of particles in the rings, by size.

- Explore the characteristics of the ring systems, including density, size, distribution, and particle composition. This can also be conducted with synchronized simultaneous observation from different observation points.

- Explore features visible on on the planetary "surface"

- Map the Jovian magnetic field and trapped charged particle environment.

- Examine phenomena of opportunity, as they arise.

We decided to baseline the same hardware that we could from the Juno mission. This involved the mothership flight computers (RAD-750's), the same rocket engine, the same solar arrays and batteries. The mothership would server as a communications relay between the deployed Cubesats and Earth, using the Juno X-band system. Thus, quite a few of the mission elements had a high TRL level. There has also been a 50-unit Cubesat Constellation demonstrated in Earth orbit. We also baselined the Raspberry Pi as the Cubesat Flight Computer, and the use of NASA/GSFC's Core Flight Software and Core Flight Executive.

The low TRL items are Cubesat communication, between units, and with the mothership, rad hard software, an onboard relational database of Engineering Data Sheets, and the P-POD architecture is of concern, since it has only operated in Earth orbit at the moment. We believe, for the same size and weight, we would have a more capable and a more agile approach to explore the mysteries of Jupiter with this approach.

Complexity

Complexity is the enemy of successful projects. It appears in the hardware and software design. Complexity comes about because we are seeking to solve bigger problems. It is related to the number of parts, and the number of interaction between parts. We can predict faults and failures from the measure of the complexity of a system.

Complexity is our enemy, but we've solved all the easy problems.

There was a 2009 study of the Complexity of Flight Software with Headquarters and most of the Field Centers participating. The sponsor was the NASA Office of the Chief Engineer. There charter was to "Bring forward deployable technical and managerial strategies to effectively address risks from growth in size and complexity of flight software."

The first issue addressed was that of growth in flight software size. They had plotted mission software size in terms of lines of code pr year of mission, and gotten an exponential growth curve, with a 10x growth every 10 years, from 1968 to 2004. they had seen similar growth curves in Defense Systems, aircraft, and automobiles.

Software size, in terms of lines of code, is an indicator of complexity. Not a great indicator, but certainly one that can be measured.

Then, they set off to define complexity of software. This involves not only the number of components of a system, but also their inter-relationships. This leads to that fact that a systems has a certain essential complexity, which comes from the problem being addressed. There is also extraneous or incidental complexity, that gets added because of the solution chosen. Essential complexity comes from the problem domain and the requirements. The only way to reduce it is to downscope the problem. It can be moved later to operations, but not erased.

One of the major finding was that "Engineers and scientists often don't realize the downstream complexity entailed by their decisions." It was also noted that "...NPR 7123, NASA System Engineering Requirements, specifies in an appendix of "best typical practices" that requirements include rationale, but offers no guidance on how to write a good rationale or check it."

One good recommendation was that Software Architecture was a little-known or well understood element of software design, but an essential one. Another finding, in the NASA context, was that often a specific optimized design vastly increases operational complexity. Incidental complexity, though, comes from design choices.

They found that COTS software was a mixed blessing, in that it comes with features not needed. Although not needed, these features require additional testing, and increase the complexity. And, it is more complex to understand and remove them, then to test them.

One of the "take-away" messages was that flight software is increasing in complexity because we are solving increasing complex problems. One solution is to address complexity with architecture.

They quote a 1968 NATO report with the same concerns for the same reasons, although they considered 10,000 lines of code as complex, then.

NASA recommended more emphasis on Fault Detection and containment.

They defined these characteristics for Flight Software:

"No direct user interfaces such as monitor and keyboard. All interactions are through uplink and downlink.

Interfaces with numerous flight hardware devices such as thrusters, reaction wheels, star trackers, motors, science instruments, temperature sensors, etc.

Executes on radiation-hardened processors and microcontrollers that are relatively slow and memory-limited. (Big source of incidental complexity)

Performs real-time processing. Must satisfy numerous timing constraints (timed commands, periodic deadlines, async event response). Being late = being wrong."

An interesting chart derived for JPL Missions (planetary) shows a vertical axis of software size times processor speed (bytes, mips) and a horizontal axis of time, where the curve through various missions is linear; ie, exponential growth, with a doubling time under two years.

The study pointed out that each step of the life cycle process, requirements, design, coding and testing, both removed defects, and inserted new one. Thus, there are residual defects that ship with the system. Some of these are never found.

We can focus on reducing the defect insertion rate, or increasing the removal rate, but the bad news is, we'll never drive the rate to zero. Thus, there will be residual defects at launch. From empirical evidence, 1 million lines of code will have 900 benign defects, 90 medium level, and 9 potentially fatal. This is based on a count of 1 residual defect per 1000 lines of code, an across-industries average for embedded code. What this leads us to conclude is that there is a current upper limit to system software complexity, measured in lines of code, because, beyond a certain size, the probability of mission failure tends to 1.

Architecture of a embedded or flight system is an essential part of the development process. Architecture tells us what we are building, not necessarily how. The architecture phase of system engineering has been slow to be adopted. The principles noted are that:

- "Architecture is an abstraction of a system that suppresses some details.
- Architecture is concerned with the public interfaces of elements and how they interact at runtime.
- Systems comprise more than one structure, e.g., runtime processes, synchronization relations, work breakdown, etc. No single structure is adequate.
- Every software system has an architecture, whether or not documented, hence the importance of architecture documentation.
- The externally visible behavior of each element is part of the architecture, but not the internal implementation details.
- The definition is indifferent as to whether the architecture is good or bad, hence the importance of architecture evaluation."

As things get more and more complex, even everyday things, we need to develop better ways to develop and verify software, whether it flys in space, or runs on our phone. Whether we are working with systems, hardware, or software, we need to bound and control the complexity.

Aerospace Failure Case Studies

Why do we study failures? It is less painful to learn from others' failures, than your own. It is critical to document failures, after a "post-mortem" analysis. Pass this information along.

There are some common traits we can identify and apply to all system accidents: improper or non-complete requirements, defective architecture or design, complacency about existing safety measures, incomplete testing, and management failures.

A defective design is the root cause of most space accidents. The nature of the defect is usually obvious in hindsight. The use of a 17 PSI pure oxygen atmosphere during a ground test in case of Apollo 1, the imperfect sealing properties of Shuttle Challenger's solid rocket booster's O-rings are both examples of this.

But a defective design can be identified and corrected before it leads to an accident thanks to quality assurance and analysis of flight parameters during testing and operation of any space hardware. This is where complacency comes into play. Disastrous accidents involving complex systems are always preceded by so-called accident precursors, which take the form of parameters out of tolerance. People responsible for those systems become accustomed to the idea that nothing bad will ever happen because nothing bad has happened yet. A routine inspection of Columbia's ill-fated launch footage performed just a few hours after the launch revealed a foam strike. Mission Control dismissed the strike because the phenomenon had been seen before. The Columbia Accident Investigation Board indeed revealed that every single Shuttle launch presented a certain measure of foam shedding from the External Tank; and even though a precise requirement was set about the tolerance for such foam shedding, the tolerance was simply increased to accommodate the measurements.

It takes a serious management failure to allow a complex organization to become accustomed to the warning signals of a defective design. This failure is often the consequences of pressure to keep up with unrealistic schedules or budgets. When the space Shuttle was first introduced, NASA management claimed it had a reliability of 1 accident in 100,000 flights. After the Challenger Accident, it turned out that the engineering community believed that the reliability was a much more realistically 1 in 100 flights. The engineering community knew about potential issues with the O-rings, but their warnings had not been properly communicated to the management, and even when they did, they were systematically ignored. Every single space disaster, presents a similar set of conditions. That is why we do a post mortem analysis. Hindsight is 20/20.

Some examples of past failures in space follow.

Mars Climate Orbiter

The spacecraft was lost on Mars in September 1999. The requirements did not specify units, so JPL used SI (metric) units and the contractor Lockheed Martin used English units. This was not caught in the review process, and led to the loss of the $125 million mission. The spacecraft crashed due to a navigation error.

The computer architecture is a single RAD6000 cpu, with 128 megabytes of ram, and 18 megabytes of flash memory, from Wind River systems, was the operating system with flight software developed at Lockheed Martin Corporation.

Sensors and Actuators included dual 3-axis gyros, a star tracker, dual sun sensors, eight thrusters, and four reaction wheels. An interesting error source in using 3 axis gyros (or other 3-axis devices such as magnetic torquer bars) is the naming of the axis. Every one has to agree on the names of the axes. Roll, pitch, yaw, x, y, z...all the data bases have to be consistent, and we all have to be on the same page. This error is usually caught in testing. Oh, and not relevant to Mars, as it has no real magnetic pole, but you did know the Earth's magnetic pole is at the geographic south pole, right?

The primary cause of this discrepancy was human error. Specifically, the flight system software on the Mars Climate Orbiter was written to calculate thruster performance using the metric unit Newtons (N), while the ground crew was entering course correction and thruster data using the Imperial measure Pound-force (lbf). This error has since been known as the *metric mix-up* and has been carefully avoided in all missions since by NASA.

"The root cause of the loss of the spacecraft was the failed translation of English units into metric units in a segment of ground-based, navigation-related mission software, as NASA has previously announced," said Arthur Stephenson, chairman of the Mars Climate Orbiter Mission Failure Investigation Board. "The failure review board has identified other significant factors that allowed this error to be born, and then let it linger and propagate to the point where it resulted in a major error in our understanding of the spacecraft's path as it approached Mars."

Reference: http://mars.jpl.nasa.gov/msp98/orbiter/

Mars Rover Pathfinder

The computer in the Mars Rover Pathfinder suffered a series of resets while on the Martian surface.
The cpu Architecture was a single RS-6000 cpu, with 1553 and VMEbuses. The Software was the VxWorks operating system, with application code in c. Sensors and Actuators included Sun sensors, a star tracker, a radar altimeter, accelerometers, and the wheel drive.

The Root Cause was Priority Inversion in the operating system. Preemptive priority thread scheduling was used. The watchdog timer caught the failure of a task to run to completion, and caused the reset. This was a sequence of tasks not exercised during testing. The problem was debugged from Earth, and a correction uploaded.

The failure was identified by the spacecraft as a failure of one task to complete its execution before the other task started. The reaction to this by the spacecraft was to reset the computer. This reset reinitializes all of the hardware and software. It also terminates the execution of the current ground commanded activities.

The failure turned out to be a case of priority inversion (how this was discovered and corrected is a fascinating story – see refs.) The higher priority task was blocked by the much lower priority task that was holding a shared resource. The lower priority task had acquired this resource and then been preempted by several of the medium priority tasks. When the higher priority task was activated, to setup the transactions for the next databus cycle, it detected that the lower priority task had not completed its execution. The resource that caused this problem was a mutual exclusion semaphore used to control access to the list of file descriptors that the select() mechanism was to wait on.

The Select mechanism creates a mutex to protect the "wait list" of file descriptors for those devices which support select. The vxWorks pipe() mechanism is such a device and the IPC mechanism used is based on using pipes. The lower priority task had called Select, which had called other tasks, which were in the process of giving the mutex semaphore. The lower priority task was preempted and the operation was not completed. Several medium priority tasks ran until the higher priority task was activated. The low priority task attempted to send the newest high priority data via the IPC mechanism which called a write routine. The write routine blocked, taking control of the mutex semaphore. More of the medium priority tasks ran, still not allowing the high priority task to run, until the low priority task was awakened. At that point, the scheduling task determined that the low priority task had not completed its cycle (a hard deadline in the system) and declared the error that initiated the reset.

References

http://www.nasa.gov/mission_pages/mars-pathfinder/
http://research.microsoft.com/en-

us/um/people/mbj/Mars_Pathfinder/

Phobos-Grunt

In November of 2010, the Russian Space Agency launched an ambitious mission to set a probe down on the small Martian moon Phobos, collect samples, and return them to Earth. There was a failure of the spacecraft propulsion system that stranded the mission in Earth orbit. It re-entered the Earth's atmosphere in January 2011.

Various causes were postulated for the failure, including interference by U.S. Radar, cosmic ray induced upsets, programming errors, and counterfeit chips. The final report from Roscosmos cited software errors, failure of chips in the electronics, possibly due to radiation damage, and the use of non-flight qualified electronics, with inadequate ground testing.

Evidently, identical chips in two assemblies failed nearly simultaneously, so quickly that an error message was not generated. It was possible that the error was recoverable, as the spacecraft entered a safe mode with a proper sun orientation for maximum power. However, the design precluded the reset mode before the spacecraft left its parking orbit. This was major design oversight.

The identified chips that failed were 512k SRAM (static random access memory. The part numbers from the Russian report were checked by NASA's Jet Propulsion Lab, and were found to be among the most radiation susceptible chips they had ever seen. Bad choice. The chips could last in space a few days, and were barely acceptable for non-critical applications, The probably failure cause was single event latch-up, which is sometimes recoverable. In single event latch up, there is a single particle strike that latches up a transistor, preventing it from operating. Usually, if you turn it off and back on again, it will work. A lot of radiation damage to the underlying semiconductor lattice fixes itself after a while, a process called "annealing."

References
Klotz, Irene "Programming Error Doomed Russian Mars Probe," Discovery News, Feb. 7, 2012, news.discovery.com

de Carbonnel, Alissa "Russia races to salvage stranded Mars probe, " Reuters, 2011. www.reuters.com
Amos, Jonathan "Phobos-Grunt mars Probe loses its way just after launch," 9 Nov. 2011, BBC News, www.bbc.co.uk

Oberg, James "Did Bad memory chips Down Russia's Mars Probe?," Feb 2012, IEEE Spectrum, IEEE.org.

Friedman, Louis D. "Phobos-Grunt Failure Report Released," 2/6/2012,
www.planetary.org/blogs/guest-blogs/lou-friedman

Phobos fail: What really happened to Russia's Mars Probe, Jan 19, 2012, RT.com.

Satellite on-orbit collision

A collision between two satellites occurred in February of 2009. One was a Russian Strela-class military satellite, massing 950 kilograms. The other was the commercial Iridium 33 communications satellite. What was the cause? They were in the same place at the same time. The Russian spacecraft had been deactivated, and was classified as space debris. The Iridium was operational, and was destroyed.

And, the bad news is, the collision created a thousand pieces of space debris larger than 4 inches, and many more smaller ones. In March 2012, a piece of the KOSMOS 2251 passed by the International Space Station, prompting the crew to take refuge in the attached Soyuz return craft as a precaution. The ISS frequently does obstacle avoidance maneuvers.

If you have problems and failures, analyze them and write them up. Take corrective action, if possible. I can assure you that if you don't and I find out, your disaster will be highlighted in my next book.

Wrap-up

Cubesats are the future. They present an opportunity to save money by standardization. This follows an old program (MMS – Multimission Modular Spacecraft) for NASA's unmanned spacecraft, which built the "bus" out of three standard modules, power, attitude control and data handling, and power. These modules were shuttle compatible for launch and recovery. The Hubble space telescope was serviced in this manner, saving a valuable on-orbit resource. Cubesats are idea for exploring more of our solar system that we can afford to do, in time and money, with large missions.

Cubesat Conferences

There are numerous Cubesat Conferences every year, and all across the globe.

Here are some examples:

- The 13th Annual CubeSat Developer's Workshop held April 20-22, 2016 in San Luis Obispo, California, USA. In 2017, tis workshop will have its 13th annual meeting.
- Interplanetary Cubesat Workshop, Cambridge, U.K., May 2017.
- European Cubesat symposium, January/February, various locations
- IAA Conference on University Satellite Missions and CubeSat Workshop Rome; Italy.
- ESA CubeSat Workshop, various European locations.
- 6U CubeSat Low Cost Space Missions Workshop, July 2012, Canberra, Australia.
- Summer CubeSat Developers' Workshop, Utah State University Campus, Logan, USA .

- Pico- and Nano-Satellite Workshop, Universität Würzburg, Würzburg, Germany.
- Winter Cubesat workshop, Jan/Feb, alternates between the University of Rome and the von Karman Institute in Brussels.
- Spring Cubesat workshop, (This is the original and main CubeSat workshop held in April at CalPoly, San Luis Obispo, the home of the CubeSat standard)
- Summer Cubesat workshop, held the weekend before SmallSat in August, Utah State University.
- Interplanetary CubeSat Workshop, spring, previously at Ithaca, NY and Boston, MA. Cambridge, U.K., May 2017.

This is by no means an exhaustive list.

Large Conferences that have Cubesat sessions:
- AAS GNC ('GN Ski') ; Brown Space Horizons Workshop
- IEEE Aerospaceresearch – Satellite
- Toulouse Space Show; SpaceOps; International Planetary Probe Workshop
- COSPAR
- SmallSat; GNC
- International Astronautical Congress
- Nanosatellite Symposium

The go-to places to start include www.cubesat.org and www.smallsat.org. NASA also sponsors a series of Cubesat workshops.

Organizations offering Cubesat Launch Services

This is not an exhaustive list.
- Innovative Solutions in Space (ISIS) – www.isispace.nl

- NanoRacks – www.nanoracks.com

- Spaceflight Industries, Inc. www.spaceflight.com

- TriSept Corporation - www.triSept.com

- Tyvak - www.tyvak.com/tls

Regulators

These government bodies have oversight on some aspects of the Cubesat. These are U. S. organization. Check the equivalent organizations in your country.

- The International Radio Amateur Union, http://www.iaru.org/satellite.html

- International Telecommunications Union, http://www.itu.int/en/Pages/default.aspx

- Space Frequency Coordination Group, https://www.sfcgonline.org/home.aspx

- Federal Communications Commission, http://wireless.fcc.gov/services/index.htm?job=service_home&id=amateur

- National Telecommunications & Information Administration, https://www.ntia.doc.gov/page/2011/manual-regulations-and-procedures-federal-radio-frequency-management-redbook

- U. S. Department of State, http://pmddtc.state.gov/

References

Antunes, Dr. Sandy, *Surviving Orbit the DIY Way: Testing the Limits Your Satellite Can and Must Match,* 2012 , Maker Media, Inc., ISBN-449310621.

Antunes, Dr. Sandy, *DIY Instruments for Amateur Space: Inventing Utility for Your Spacecraft Once It Achieves Orbit,* Maker Media, Inc., ISBN-978-1449310646.

Antunes, Dr. Sandy, *DIY Comms and Control for Amateur Space: Talking and Listening to Your Satellite,* 2015, Maker Media, Inc., ISBN-978-1449310660.

Antunes, Dr. Sandy, *DIY Satellite Platforms: Building a Space-Ready General Base Picosatellite for Any Mission,* 2012, Maker Media, Inc. ISBN-978-1449310608.]

Asmar, Sami; Matousek, Steve "Mars Cube One (MarCO), First Planetary CubeSat Mission (presentation), 2014, JPL, avail: www.jpl.nasa.gov/cubesat/missions/marco.php

Avery, Keith; Fenchel, Jeffery; Mee, Jesse; Kemp, William; Netzer. Richard; Elkins, Donald; Zufelt, Brian; Alexander, David; *"Total Dose Test Results for Cubesat Electronics,"* 2011 IEEE Radiation Effects Data Workshop, 25-29 July 2011, Las Vegas, NV, pp. 1-8, 978-1-4577-1281-4. avail: www.cosmiacpubs.org/pubs/TDTRCE.pdf

Cudmore, Alan NASA/GSFC's Flight Software Architecture: core Flight Executive and Core Flight System, NASA/GSFC Code 582.

Datta, Lakshya Vaibhav, Guven Ugur (Ed*) Introduction to Nanosatellite Technology and Components: Applications of Cubesat Technology,* 2012, Lambert Academic Publishing, ISBN-978-3847314196.

DeCoursey, R.; Melton, Ryan; Estes, Robert R. Jr. "Sensors,

Systems, and Next-Generation Satellites X," Proceedings of the SPIE, Vol. 6361 pp 63611m (2006). (use of non-radiation hardened cpus).

De Selding Peter B. "1 in 5 Cubesats Violates International Disposal Guidelines," 2015. available, http://spacenews.com/1-in-5-Cubesats-violate-international-orbit-disposal-guidelines/

Dreißas, Riccardo *Cubesat electrical power system simulation: a generic approach*, 2013, AV Akademikerverlag, ISBN-978-3639473766.

Dunn, William R. *Practical Design of Safety-Critical Computer Systems*, July 2002, Springer, ISBN-0971752702.

Eickhoff, Jens *Onboard Computers, Onboard Software and Satellite Operations: An Introduction*, 2011, Springer Aerospace Technology, ISBN-3642251692.

Engineering and Medicine, National Academies of Sciences (Author), Division on Engineering and Physical Sciences (Author), Space Studies Board (Author), *Achieving Science with Cubesats: Thinking Inside the Box,* National Academies Press, 2016, ISBN-978-0309442633.

Fortescue, Peter and Stark, John *Spacecraft System Engineering*, 2nd ed, Wiley, 1995, ISBN 0-471-95220-6.

Fowler, Kim *Mission-Critical and Safety-Critical Systems Handbook: Design and Development for Embedded Applications,* Newnes; 1st edition, November 20, 2009, ISBN-0750685670.

Harland, David M. and Lorenz, Ralph D. *Space Systems Failures, Disasters and Rescues of Satellites, Rockets and Space Probes,*. 2005, Praxis Publishing, ISBN 0-387-21519-0.

Holmes-Siedle, A. G. and Adams, L. *Handbook of Radiation Effects*, 2002, Oxford University Press, ISBN 0-19-850733-X.

Kalinsky, David, "Architecture of Safety-Critical Systems," Aug 23. 2005, available white paper at www.embedded.com.

Kerber, Jonathas G. "An Introduction to Cubesats as Teaching Tools and Technology Testing Platforms, University of Ottawa.

Klofas, Bryan, "Frequency Allocation for Government-funded Cubesats: NSF Paves the Way, 2011, avail: klofas.com/papers/klofas_nsf_comm_amsat2011.pdf

Krämer, Bernd J. and Völker, Norbert (Eds.) *Safety-Critical Real-Time Systems*, 2010, ISBN-10-1441950192.

Lappas, Vaios, et al *CubeSail: A low cost Cubesat based solar sail demonstration mission*, Advances in Space Research, 2001, 48.11, 1890-1901.

Leveson, Nancy G. "Software Safety in Embedded Computer Systems," Communications of the ACM. Vol. 34, No. 2, February 1991. pp. 34-46.

Leveson, Nancy G. *System Safety and Computers*, Addison-Wesley, 1995, ISBN 0-201-11972-2.

Logsdon, Tom *Orbital Mechanics: Theory and Applications*, 1997, Wiley-Interscience, ISBN 0471146366.

Mahdi, Mohammed Chessab *Introduction to Cubesat Technology and Subsystem: Orbit Design, Debris Impact, and Orbital Decay Prediction,* Lambert Academic Publishing, 2016, ISBN-978-3659960710.

Madni, Mohamed Atef; Raad, Raad; Tubbal, Faisal "Inter-CubeSat Communications: Routing Between
CubeSat Swarms in a DTN Architecture," presentation, avail:https://icubesat.org/papers/2015-2/2015-b-2-1

Maurer, Richard H.; Fraeman, Martin E.; Martin, Mark N.; Roth,

David R. "Harsh Environments: Space Radiation Environment, Effects, and Mitigation, The Johns Hopkins University, Applied Physics Laboratory, Technical Digest, Vol 28, No. 1, 2008.

Messenger, G. C. and Ash, M. S. *The Effects of Radiation on Electronic Systems,* 1992, Van Nostrand Reinhold.

Mikaelian, Tsoline "Spacecraft Charging and Hazards to Electronics in Space" May 2001, avail: https://www.researchgate.net/publication/45858016_Spacecraft_Charging_and_Hazards_to_Electronics_in_Space.

Petersen, Edward *Single Event Effects in Aerospace* 1st Ed. Wiley-IEEE Press; 1 edition, October 4, 2011, ISBN- 0470767499.

Petro, Andrew "Small Spacecraft Technology, Briefing to NASA Advisory Committee, April 15, 2014," https://www.nasa.gov/sites/default/files/files/APetro_SmallSpacecraft.pdf .

Prussing, John R and Conway, Bruce A. *Orbital Mechanics*, 1993, Oxford University Press, ISBN- 0195078349.

Sahu, Kusum, *EEE-INST-002, Instructions for EEE Parts Selection, Screening, Qualification, and Derating*, with addendum 1, April 2008, NASA/TP-2003-212242.

Schaire, Scott "NASA Near Earth Network (NEN) and Space Network (SN) Support of Cubesat Communications, March, 2016, avail: https://ntrs.nasa.gov/search.jsp?R=20160005439

Stakem, Patrick H. "Linux in Space", Oct. 2, 2003, invited presentation, Institution of Electrical Engineers, Sheffield Hallam University, Sheffield, UK.

Stakem, Patrick H. "The Applications of Computers and Microprocessors Onboard Spacecraft, NASA/GSFC 1980.

Stakem, Patrick H. "Free Software in Space–the NASA Case,"

invited paper, Software Livre 2002, May 3, 2002, Porto Allegre, Brazil.

Stakem, Patrick H., Korol, Guilherme, Gomes, Gabriel Augusto, "A Lightweight Open Source Command and Control Center and its Interface to Cubesat Flight Software." Presented at Flight Software-15 Conference (FSW-15), The Johns Hopkins University, Applied Physics Laboratory.

Stakem, Patrick H.; Rezende, Aryadne; Ravazzi, Andre "Cubesat Swarm Communications," 2016.

Stakem, Patrick H.; Da Costa, Rodrigo Santos Valente; Rezende, Aryasdne; Ravazzi, Andre "A Cubesat-based alternative for the Juno Mission to Jupiter, 2017, available form the author, pstakem@jhu.edu.

Stakem, Patrick H., Kerber, Jonathas "Rad-hard software, Cubesat Flight Computer Self-monitoring, Testing, Diagnosis, and Remediation," 2017, available from the author, pstakem1@jhu.edu.

Stakem, Patrick H. "Lunar and Planetary Cubesat Missions," March Volume 15, Polytech Revista de Tecnologia e Ciência, avail: http://www.polyteck.com.br/revista_online/ed_15.pdf

Stakem, Patrick H. "Lunar and Planetary Cubesat Missions," March Volume 15, Polytech Revista de Tecnologia e Ciência, avail: http://www.polyteck.com.br/revista_online/ed_15.pdf

Swartwout, Michael *The First One Hundred Cubesats: A Statistical Loo*k, JoSS, Vol. 2, No. 2, pp. 213-233.

Swartwout, Michael "The Long-Threatened Flood of University-Class Spacecraft (and Cubesats) Has Come: Analyzing the Numbers"
Avail: digitalcommons.usu.edu/cgi/viewcontent.cgi?article=2972&contex

t=smallsat

Truszkowski, Walt; Hallock, Harold L.; Rouff, Christopher; Karlin, Jay; Rash, Hinchey, Mike; Sterritt, Roy *Autonomous and Automatic Systems,: With Applications to NASA Intelligent Spacecraft Operations and Exploration* Systems, Monographs in System and Software Engineering, Springer, 009, ISBN 9781846282331.

Truszkowski, Walt; Clark, P. E.; Curtis, S.; Rilee, M. Marr, G. A*NTS: Exploring the Solar System with an Autonomous Nanotechnology Swarm.* J. Lunar and Planetary Science XXXIII (2002).

Violette, Daniel P. "Arduino/Raspberry Pi: Hobbyist Hardware and Radiation Total Dose Degradation," 2014, presented at the EEE Parts for Small Missions Conference, NASA-GSFC, Greenbelt, MD, September 10-11, 2014.

Welti, C. Robert, , *Satellite Basics for Everyone: An Illustrated Guide to Satellites for Non-Technical and Technical People,* iUniverse, 2012, ASIN-B008I21XW6.

Wertz, James R. (ed) *Spacecraft Attitude Determination and Control,* section 6.9, Onboard Computers, 1980, Kluwer, ISBN 90-277-1204-2.

Wichmann, Brian A. *Software in Safety Related Systems,* Wiley, 1992. ISBN 0471-93474-7.

Wikipedia, various.

Wooster, Paul; Boswell, David; Stakem, Patrick; Cowan-Sharp, Jessy "Open Source Software for Small Satellites," SSC07-XII-3, 21st. Annual AIAA/USU, paper SSC07-XII-3, July 2007.

Resources

Small Spacecraft Technology State of the Art, NASA-Ames, NASA/TP2014-216648/REV1, July 2014.

Core Flight System (CFS) Deployment Guide, Ver. 2.8, 9/30/2010, NASA/GSFC 582-2008-012.

NASA Systems Engineering Handbook, NASA/SP-2007-6105, Rev. 1. (available on Google Books, Amazon, and others)

Cubesat Design Specification, Cubesat Program, California Polytechnic State University, avail:
https://www.google.com/search?q=Cubesat+Design+Specification&ie=utf-8&oe=utf-8
and at www.Cubesat.org

Cubesat Concept and the Provision of Deployer Services, avail:
https://eoportal.org/web/eoportal/satellite-missions/content/-/article/Cubesat-concept-1

NASA systems Engineering Handbook, NASA SP-2007-6105. Avail:
https://ntrs.nasa.gov/archive/nasa/casi.ntrs.nasa.gov/20080008301.pdf

www.ccsds.org

https://nasasearch.nasa.gov/

Here is a 3-D model of a Cubesat that you can download, print on heavy cardstock, and assemble.
http://www.space.aau.dk/Cubesat/kits.html

Spacetrack.org (requires an account)

http://www.celestrak.com/NORAD/elements/

http://satellitedebris.net/Database/

NASA, Software Documentation Standard, NASA-STD-2100-91, available:
https://ntrs.**nasa**.gov/archive/**nasa**/casi.ntrs.**nasa**.gov/19980228459.pdf

Interplanetary Cubesats: Opening the Solar System to a Broad Community at Lower Cost; JPL, 2012, avail:
https://www.nasa.gov/pdf/716078main_Staehle_2011_PhI_**Cubesat**.pdf

Cubesat: A new Generation of Picosatellite for Education and Industry Low-Cost Space Experimentation, 14th Annual/USU Conference on Small Satellites.
Avail: digitalcommons.usu.edu/cgi/viewcontent.cgi?article=2069&context=smallsat

MakerSat: A Cubesat Designed for In-Space 3D Print and Assembly, SSC16-WK-29,
avail: digitalcommons.usu.edu/cgi/viewcontent.cgi?article=3444&context=smallsat

Cubesat Design Specification (CDS) Rev. 13, Cubesat Program, Cal Poly. Avail: http://www.Cubesat.org/

NASA, John F. Kennedy Space Center, Launch Services Program, Program Level Dispenser and Cubesat Requirements Document, LSP-REQ-317.01, Rev. B, Jan. 2014.

Guidance on Obtaining Licenses for Small Satellites, Federal Communications Commission, March 15, 2013, 13-445. avail:
https://www.fcc.gov/document/guidance-obtaining-licenses-small-satellites

Amateur Radio Satellite Organization (AMSAT) – www.amsat.org

Launch Services Program, Program Level Dispenser and Cubesat Requirements Document, NASA, John F. Kennedy Space Center, LSP-REQ-317.01, Rev. B. avail: www.nasa.gov/pdf/627972main_LSP-REQ-317_01A.pdf

General Payload Users Guide, Spaceflight, Inc. SF-2100-PUG-00001, www.spaceflightindustries.com

NASA Open Source Agreement, avail: https://opensource.org/licenses/NASA-1.3

InterPlanetary Networking Special Interest Group (IPNSIG) - http://ipnsig.org/

CubeSat: A new Generation of Picosatellite for Education and Industry Low-Cost Space Experimentation, avail: users.csc.calpoly.edu/~csturner/ssc01.pdf

Rapid Build and Space Qualification of Cubesats, avail: www.digitalcommons.usu.edu/cgi/viewcontent.cgi?article=1148&context=smallsat

Open Source Engineering Tools
http://wiki.developspace.net/Open_Source_Engineering_Tools

100 Earth Shattering Remote Sensing Applications and Uses, 2015, GIS Geography
avail: http://gisgeography.com/100-earth-remote-sensing-applications-uses/

Report Concerning Space Data Systems Standards, Mission Operations Services Concept, CCSDS Informational Report, CCSDS 520.0-G-3, Green Book, December 2010, avail, ccsds.org

Overview of Space Communications Protocols
Avail: cwe.ccsds.org/sls/docs/SLS.../130x0g2_master_Dec16_2013.docx

Core Flight System – http://cfs.gsfc.nasa.gov

https://cubesatcookbook.com

https://cubesatcookbook.com

http://pmddtc.state.gov/

http://srag-nt.jsc.nasa.gov/SpaceRadiation/What/What.cfm

Glossary

1553 – Military standard data bus, serial, 1 Mbps.
1U – one unit for a Cubesat, 10 x 10 x 10 cm.
3U – three units for a Cubesat
6u – 6 units in size, where 1u is defined by dimensions and weight.
802.11 – a radio frequency wireless data communications standard.
AACS – (JPL) Attitude and articulation control system.
ACE – attitude control electronics
Actuator – device which converts a control signal to a mechanical action.
Ada – a computer language.
A/D, ADC – analog to digital converter
AEB -
AFB – Air Force Base.
AGC – Automated guidance and control.
AIAA – American Institute of Aeronautics and Astronautics.
AIST – NASA GSFC Advanced Information System Technology.
ALU – arithmetic logic unit.
AmSat – Amateur Satellite. Favored by Ham Radio operators as communication relays.
Analog – concerned with continuous values.
ANSI – American National Standards Institute
Android – an operating system based on Gnu-Linux, popular for smart phones and tablet computers.
Antares – Space launch vehicle, compatible with Cubesats, by Orbital/ATK (U.S.)
AP – application programs.
API – application program interface; specification for software modules to communicate.
APL – Applied Physics Laboratory, of the Johns Hopkins University.
Apm – antenna pointing mechanism
Apollo – US manned lunar program.
Arduino – a small, inexpensive microcontroller architecture.
Arinc – Aeronautical Radio, Inc. commercial company supporting transportation, and providing standards for avionics.
ARM – Acorn RISC machine; a 32-bit architecture with wide

application in embedded systems.
ARPA – (U. S.) Advanced Research Projects Agency.
ArpaNet – Advanced Research Projects Agency (U.S.), first packet switched network, 1968.
ASIC – application specific integrated circuit
async – non synchronized
ATAC – Applied Technologies Advanced Computer.
ATP – authority to proceed
AU – astronomical unit. Roughly 93 million miles, the mean distance between Earth and Sun,
BAE – British Aerospace.
Baud – symbol rate; may or may not be the same as bit rate.
BCD – binary coded decimal. 4-bit entity used to represent 10 different decimal digits; with 6 spare states.
Beowolf – a cluster of commodity computers; multiprocessor, using Linux.
Big-endian – data format with the most significant bit or byte at the lowest address, or transmitted first.
Binary – using base 2 arithmetic for number representation.
BIST – built-in self test.
Bit – binary variable, value of 1 or 0.
Boolean – a data type with two values; an operation on these data types; named after George Boole, mid-19th century inventor of Boolean algebra.
Bootloader – initial program run after power-on or reset. Gets the computer up & going.
Bootstrap – a startup or reset process that proceeds without external intervention.
BSD – Berkeley Software Distribution version of the Bell Labs Unix operating system.
BP - bundle protocol, for dealing with errors and disconnects.
BSP – board support package. Customization Software and device drivers.
Buffer – a temporary holding location for data.
Bug – an error in a program or device.
Bus – an electrical connection between 2 or more units; the engineering part of the spacecraft.
byte – a collection of 8 bits

C – programming language from Bell Labs, circa 1972.
cache – temporary storage between cpu and main memory.
Cache coherency – process to keep the contents of multiple caches consistent,
CalPoly – California Polytechnic State University,. San Luis Obispo, CA.
CAN - controller area network bus.
CCSDS – Consultive Committee on Space Data Systems.
CDR – critical design review
C&DH – Command and Data Handling
CDFP CCSDS File Delivery Protocol
cFE – Core Flight Executive – NASA GSFC reusable flight software.
CFS – Core Flight System – NASA GSFC reusable flight software.
Chip – integrated circuit component.
Clock – periodic timing signal to control and synchronize operations.
CME – Coronal Mass Ejection. Solar storm.
CMOS – complementary metal oxide semiconductor; a technology using both positive and negative semiconductors to achieve low power operation.
CogE – cognizant engineer for a particular discipline; go-to guy; specialist.
Complement – in binary logic, the opposite state.
Compilation – software process to translate source code to assembly or machine code (or error codes).
Configware – equivalent of software for FPGA architectures; configuration information.
Constellation – a grouping of satellites.
Control Flow – computer architecture involving directed flow through the program; data dependent paths are allowed.
COP – computer operating properly.
Coprocessor – another processor to supplement the operations of the main processor. Used for floating point, video, etc. Usually relies on the main processor for instruction fetch; and control.
Cordic – Coordinate Rotation Digital Computer – to calculate hyberbolic and trig functions.

Cots – commercial, off the shelf
CPU – central processing unit
CRC – cyclic redundancy code – error detection and correction mechanism.
Cubesat – small inexpensive satellite for colleges, high schools, and individuals.
D/A – digital to analog conversion.
DAC – digital to analog converter.
Daemon – in multitasking, a program that runs in the background.
DARPA – Defense advanced research projects agency.
Dataflow – computer architecture where a changing value forces recalculation of dependent values.
Datagram – message on a packet switched network; the delivery, arrival time, and order of arrival are not guaranteed.
dc – direct current.
D-cache – data cache.
DDR – dual data rate memory.
Deadlock – a situation in which two or more competing actions are each waiting for the other to finish, and thus neither ever does.
DCE – data communications equipment; interface to the network.
Deadly embrace – a deadlock situation in which 2 processes are each waiting for the other to finish.
Denorm – in floating point representation, a non-zero number with a magnitude less than the smallest normal number.
Device driver – specific software to interface a peripheral to the operating system.
Digital – using discrete values for representation of states or numbers.
Dirty bit – used to signal that the contents of a cache have changed.
Discrete – single bit signal.
DMA – direct memory access.
Dnepr – Russian space launch system compatible with Cubesats.
DOD – (U. S.) Department of Defense.
DOE – (U. S.) Department of Energy.
DOF – degrees of freedom.
Downlink – from space to earth.
Dram – dynamic random access memory.
DSP – digital signal processing/processor.

DTE – data terminal equipment; communicates with the DCE to get to the network.
DTN – delay tolerant networks.
DUT – device under test.
ECC – error correcting code
EDAC – error detecting and correction circuitry.
EDAC – error detection and correction.
EGSE – electrical ground support equipment
EIA – Electronics Industry Association.
ELV – expendable launch vehicle.
Embedded system – a computer systems with limited human interfaces and performing specific tasks. Usually part of a larger system.
EMC – electromagnetic compatibility.
EMI – electromagnetic interference.
EOL – end of life.
EOS – Earth Observation spacecraft.
Ephemeris – orbital position data.
Epitaxial – in semiconductors, have a crystalline overlayer with a well-defined orientation.
EPS – electrical power subsystem.
ESA – European Space Organization.
ESRO – European Space Research Organization
ESTO – NASA/GSFC – Earth Science Technology Office.
Ethernet – networking protocol, IEEE 802.3
ev – electron volt, unit of energy
EVA – extra-vehicular activity.
Exception – interrupt due to internal events, such as overflow.
EXPRESS racks – on the ISS, EXpedite the PRocessing of Experiments for Space Station Racks
FAA – (U S.) Federal Aviation Administration.
Fail-safe – a system designed to do no harm in the event of failure.
Falcon – launch vehicle from SpaceX.
FCC – (U.S.) Federal Communications Commission.
FDC – fault detection and correction.
Femtosatellites - smaller than a Cubesat, 3.5 cm on a side.
Firewire – IEEE-1394 standard for serial communication.
Firmware – code contained in a non-volatile memory.

Fixed point – computer numeric format with a fixed number of digits or bits, and a fixed radix point. Integers.
Flag – a binary state variable.
Flash – non-volatile memory
Flatsat – prototyping and test setup, laid out on a bench for easy access.
FlightLinux – NASA Research Program for Open Source code in space.
Floating point – computer numeric format for real numbers; has significant digits and an exponent.
FPGA – field programmable gate array.
FPU – floating point unit, an ALU for floating point numbers.
Full duplex – communication in both directions simultaneously.
Fram – ferromagnetic RAM; a non-volatile memory technology
FRR – Flight Readiness Review
FSW – flight software.
FTP – file transfer protocol
Gbyte – 109 bytes.
GEO – geosynchronous orbit.
GeV – billion (109) electron volts.
GNC – guidance, navigation, and control.
Gnu – recursive acronym, gnu is not unix.
GPIO – general purpose I/O.
GPL – gnu public license used for free software; referred to as the "copyleft."
GPS – Global Positioning system – Navigation satellites.
GPU – graphics processing unit. ALU for graphics data.
GSFC – Goddard Space Flight Center, Greenbelt, MD.
Gyro – (gyroscope) a sensor to measure rotation.
Half-duplex – communications in two directions, but not simultaneously.
HAL/S – computer language.
Handshake – co-ordination mechanism.
HDL – hardware description language
Hertz – cycles per second.
Hexadecimal – base 16 number representation.
Hi-rel – high reliability
HPCC – High Performance Computing and Communications.

Hypervisor – virtual machine manager. Can manage multiple operating systems.
I2C – a serial communications protocol.
IARU – International Amateur Radio Union
I-cache – Instruction cache.
ICD – interface control document.
IC&DH – Instrument Command & Data Handling.
IEEE – Institute of Electrical and Electronic engineers
IEEE-754 – standard for floating point representation and calculation.
IIC – inter-integrated circuit (I/O).
IMU – inertial measurement unit.
INPE Instituto Nacional de Pesquisas Espaciais (Brazilian National Institute for Space Research)
Integer – the natural numbers, zero, and the negatives of the natural numbers.
Interrupt – an asynchronous event to signal a need for attention (example: the phone rings).
Interrupt vector – entry in a table pointing to an interrupt service routine; indexed by interrupt number.
IP – intellectual property; Internet protocol.
IP core – IP describing a chip design that can be licensed to be used in an FPGA or ASIC.
IP-in-Space – Internet Protocol in Space.
IR – infrared, 1-400 terahertz. Perceived as heat.
IRAD – Independent Research & Development.
ISA – instruction set architecture, the software description of the computer.
ISO – International Standards Organization.
ISR – interrupt service routine, a subroutine that handles a particular interrupt event.
ISS – International Space Station
I&T – integration & test
ITAR – International Trafficking in Arms Regulations (US Dept. of State)
ITU – International Telecommunications Union
IV&V – Independent validation and verification.
JEM – Japanese Experiment Module, on the ISS.

JHU – Johns Hopkins University.
JPL – Jet Propulsion Laboratory
JSC – Johnson Space Center, Houston, Texas.
JTAG – Joint Test Action Group; industry group that lead to IEEE 1149.1, Standard Test Access Port and Boundary-Scan Architecture.
JWST – James Webb Space Telescope – follow on to Hubble.
Kbps – kilo (103) bits per second.
Kernel – main portion of the operating system. Interface between the applications and the hardware.
Kg – kilogram.
kHz – kilo (103) hertz
KVA – kilo volts amps – a measure of electrical power
Ku band – 12-18 Ghz radio
Lan – local area network, wired or wireless
LaRC – (NASA) Langley Research Center.
Latchup – condition in which a semiconductor device is stuck in one state.
Lbf – pounds-force.
LEO – low Earth orbit.
Let- Linear Energy Transfer
Lidar – optical radar.
Linux – open source operating system.
List – a data structure.
Little-endian – data format with the least significant bit or byte at the highest address, or transmitted last.
Logic operation – generally, negate, AND, OR, XOR, and their inverses.
Loop-unrolling – optimization of a loop for speed at the cost of space.
LRR – launch readiness review
LRU – least recently used; an algorithm for item replacement in a cache.
LSB – least significant bit or byte.
LSP – (NASA) launch services program, or launch services provider
LUT – look up table.
Master-slave – control process with one element in charge. Master

status may be exchanged among elements.
Mbps – mega (106) bits per second.
Mbyte – one million (106 or 220) bytes.
Memory leak – when a program uses memory resources but does not return them, leading to a lack of available memory.
Memory scrubbing – detecting and correcting bit errors.
MEMS – Micro Electronic Mechanical System.
MESI – modified, exclusive, shared, invalid state of a cache coherency protocol.
MEV – million electron volts.
MHz – one million (106) Hertz
Microcontroller – monolithic cpu + memory + I/O.
Microkernel – operating system which is not monolithic, functions execute in user space.
Microprocessor – monolithic cpu.
Microsat – satellite with a mass between 10 and 100 kg.
Microsecond – 10-6 second.
Microkernel – operating system which is not monolithic. So functions execute in user space.
MLI – multi-layer insulation.
MPA – multiple payload adapter for deploying multiple p-pod's
MPE – Maximum predicted environments.
mram – magnetorestrictive random access memory.
mSec – Millisecond; (10-3) second.
MIPS – millions of instructions per second.
MMU – memory management unit; manned maneuvering unit.
MSB – most significant bit or byte.
Multiplex – combining signals on a communication channel by sampling.
Multicore – multiple processing cores on one substrate or chip; need not be identical.
Mutex – a software mechanism to provide mutual exclusion between tasks.
Nano – 10-9
NanoRacks – a company providing a facility onboard the ISS to support Cubesats
nanoSat – small satellite with a mass between 1 and 10 kg.
NASA - National Aeronautics and Space Administration.

NDA – non-disclosure agreement; legal agreement protecting IP.
NEN – (NASA's) Near Earth Network
Nibble – 4 bits, ½ byte.
NIST – National Institute of Standards and Technology (US), previously, National Bureau of Standards.
NMI – non-maskable interrupt; cannot be ignored by the software.
Normalized number – in the proper format for floating point representation.
NRCSD - NanoRack CubeSat Deployer
NRE – non-recurring engineering; one-time costs for a project.
NSF – (U.S.) National Science Foundation.
NSR – non-space rated.
NTIA (U.S.) National Telecommunications and Information Administration
NUMA – non-uniform memory access for multiprocessors; local and global memory access protocol.
NVM – non-volatile memory.
NWS – (U.S.) National Weather Service
Nyquist rate – in communications, the minimum sampling rate, equal to twice the highest frequency in the signal.
OBC – on board computer
OBD – On-Board diagnostics.
OBP – On Board Processor
Off-the-shelf – commercially available; not custom.
OpAmp – (Linear) operational amplifier; linear gain and isolation stage.
OpCode – encoded computer instruction.
Open source – methodology for hardware or software development with free distribution and access.
Operating system – software that controls the allocation of resources in a computer.
OSAL   operating system abstraction layer.
OSI – Open systems interconnect model for networking, from ISO.
Overflow - the result of an arithmetic operation exceeds the capacity of the destination.
Packet – a small container; a block of data on a network.
Paging – memory management technique using fixed size memory blocks.

Paradigm – a pattern or model
Paradigm shift – a change from one paradigm to another. Disruptive or evolutionary.
Parallel – multiple operations or communication proceeding simultaneously.
Parity – an error detecting mechanism involving an extra check bit in the word.
Pc – personal computer.
PC-104 – standard for a board (90 x 96 mm), and a bus for embedded use.
PCB – printed circuit board.
pci – personal computer interface (bus).
PCM – pulse code modulation.
PDR – preliminary design review
Peta - 1015 or 250
Phonesat – small satellite using a cell phone for onboard control and computation.
Picosat – small satellite with a mass between 0.1 and 1 kg.
Piezo – production of electricity by mechanical stress.
Pinout – mapping of signals to I/O pins of a device.
Pipeline – operations in serial, assembly-line fashion.
PiSat – a Cubesat architecture developed at NASA-GSFC, based on the Raspberry Pi architecture.
Pixel – picture element; smallest addressable element on a display or a sensor.
PLL – phase locked loop.
PocketQube – smaller than a Cubesat; 5 cm cubed, a mass of no more than 180 grams, and uses COTS components.
Poc – point of contact
POSIX – IEEE standard operating system.
PPF – payload processing facility
PPL – preferred parts list (NASA).
P-POD – Cubesat launch dispenser, Poly-Picosatellite Orbital Deployer
Psia – pounds per square inch, absolute.
PSP – Platform Support Package.
PWM – pulse width modulation.
Python – programming language.

Quadrature encoder – an incremental rotary encoder providing rotational position information.
Queue – first in, first out data buffer structure; implemented in hardware or software.
Rad – unit of radiation exposure
Rad750 – A radiation hardened IBM PowerPC cpu.
Radix point – separates integer and fractional parts of a real number.
RAID – redundant array of inexpensive disks.
Ram – random access memory.
RBF – remove before flight.
Real-time – system that responds to events in a predictable, bounded time.
Register – temporary storage location for a data item.
Reset – signal and process that returns the hardware to a known, defined state.
RF – radio frequency
RFC – request for comment
RISC – reduced instruction set computer.
RHPPC – Rad-Hard Power PC.
RHS – rad-hard software
RISC – reduced instruction set computer.
Router – networking component for packets.
RS-232/422/423 – asynchronous and synchronous serial communication standards.
RT – remote terminal.
RTC – real time clock.
RTOS – real time operating system.
SAM – sequential access memory, like a magnetic tape.
Sandbox – an isolated and controlled environment to run untested or potentially malicious code.
SDR – software defined radio
SDRAM – synchronous dynamic random access memory.
Segmentation – dividing a network or memory into sections.
Semiconductor – material with electrical characteristics between conductors and insulators; basis of current technology processor, memory, and I/O devices, as well as sensors.
Semaphore – a binary signaling element among processes.

SD – secure digital (non-volatile memory card).
SDVF – Software Development and Validation Facility.
Sensor – a device that converts a physical observable quantity or event to a signal.
Serial – bit by bit.
SEU – single event upset (radiation induced error).
Servo – a control device with feedback.
SIMD – single instruction, multiple data (parallel processing)
Six-pack – a six U Cubesat, 10 x 20 x 30 cm.
SMP – symmetric multiprocessing.
Snoop – monitor packets in a network, or data in a cache.
SN – (NASA's) Space Network
SOA – safe operating area; also, state of the art.
SOC – system on a chip; also state-of-charge.
Socket – an end-point in communication across a network
Soft core – a hardware description language description of a cpu core.
Software – set of instructions and data to tell a computer what to do.
SMP – symmetric multiprocessing.
Snoop – monitor packets in a network, or data in a cache.
Spacewire – high speed (160 Mbps) link.
SPI - Serial Peripheral Interface - a synchronous serial communication interface.
SRAM – static random access memory.
Stack – first in, last out data structure. Can be hardware or software.
Stack pointer – a reference pointer to the top of the stack.
STAR – self test and repair.
State machine – model of sequential processes.
STOL – system test oriented language, a scripting language for testing systems.
T&I – test and integration.
Terrabyte – 1012 bytes.
SAA – South Atlantic anomaly. High radiation zone.
SEB – single event burnout.
SEU – single event upset.
SEL – single event latchup.

Soc – state of charge; system on a chip.
Soft core – hardware description description language model of a logic core.
SOI – silicon on insulator
SoS – silicon on sapphire – an inherently radiation-hard technology
spi – serial peripheral interface
SpaceCube – an advanced FPGA-based flight computer.
SpaceWire – networking and interconnect standard.
Space-X – commercial space company.
SRAM – static random access memory.
Stack – first in, last out data structure. Can be hardware or software.
Stack pointer – a reference pointer to the top of the stack.
State machine – model of sequential processes.
SWD – serial wire debug.
Synchronous – using the same clock to coordinate operations.
System – a collection of interacting elements and relationships with a specific behavior.
System of Systems – a complex collection of systems with pooled resources.
Suitsat – old Russian spacesuit, instrumented with an 8-bit micro, and launched from the ISS.
Swarm – a collection of satellites that can operate cooperatively.
sync – synchronize, synchronized.
TCP/IP – Transmission Control Protocol/Internet protocol.
TDRSS – Tracking and Data Relay satellite system.
Tera - 1012 or 240
Test-and-set – coordination mechanism for multiple processes that allows reading to a location and writing it in a non-interruptible manner.
TCP/IP – transmission control protocol/internet protocol; layered set of protocols for networks.
Thread – smallest independent set of instructions managed by a multiprocessing operating system.
TID – total ionizing dose.
TMR – triple modular redundancy.
Toolchain – set of software tools for development.

Transceiver – receiver and transmitter in one box.
Transducer – a device that converts one form of energy to another.
Train – a series of satellites in the same or similar orbits, providing sequential observations.
TRAP – exception or fault handling mechanism in a computer; an operating system component.
Triplicate – using three copies (of hardware, software, messaging, power supplies, etc.). for redundancy and error control.
TRL – technology readiness level
Truncate – discard. cutoff, make shorter.
TT&C – tracking, telemetry, and command.
ttl – transistor-transistor logic integrated circuit.
UART – Universal asynchronous receiver-transmitter.
UDP – User datagram protocol; part of the Internet Protocol.
uM – micro (10^{-6}) meter
Underflow – the result of an arithmetic operation is smaller than the smallest representable number.
UoSat – a family of small spacecraft from Surrey Space Technology Ltd. (UK).
uplink – from ground to space.
USAF – United States Air Force.
USB – universal serial bus.
VDC – volts, direct current.
Vector – single dimensional array of values.
VHDL – very high level design language.
VIA – vertical conducting pathway through an insulating layer.
Virtual memory – memory management technique using address translation.
Virtualization – creating a virtual resource from available physical resources.
Virus – malignant computer program.
Viterbi Decoder – a maximum likelihood decoder for data encoded with a Convolutional code for error control. Can be implemented in software or hardware
VLIW – very long instruction word – mechanism for parallelism.
VxWorks – real time operating system from Wind River systems.
WiFi – short range digital radio.
Watchdog – hardware/software function to sanity check the

hardware, software, and process; applies corrective action if a fault is detected; fail-safe mechanism.

Wiki – the Hawaiian word for "quick." Refers to a collaborative content website.

Word – a collection of bits of any size; does not have to be a power of two.

Write-back – cache organization where the data is not written to main memory until the cache location is needed for re-use.

Write-through – all cache writes also go to main memory.

X-band – 7 – 11 GHz.

Xilinx – manufacturer of programmable logic and FPGA's.

Zener – voltage reference diode.

Zero address – architecture using implicit addressing, like a stack.

Zombie-sat – a dead satellite, in orbit.

Zone of Exclusion – volume in which the presence of an object or personnel, or activities are prohibited.

If you enjoyed this book, you might find something else from the author interesting as well. Available on Amazon Kindle.

16-bit Microprocessors, History and Architecture, 2013 PRRB Publishing, ASIN B00D5ETQ3U.

4- and 8-bit Microprocessors, Architecture and History, 2013, PRRB Publishing, ASIN B00D5ZSKCC.

Apollo's Computers, 2014, PRRB Publishing, ASIN B00LDT2I7.

The Architecture and Applications of the ARM Microprocessors, 2013, PRRB Publishing, ASIN B00BAFF4OQ.

Earth Rovers: for Exploration and Environmental Monitoring, 2014, PRRB Publishing, ASIN B00MBKZCBE.

Embedded Computer Systems, Volume 1, Introduction and Architecture, 2013, PRRB Publishing, ASIN B00GB0W4GG.

The History of Spacecraft Computers from the V-2 to the Space Station, 2013, PRRB Publishing, ASIN B004L626U6.

Floating Point Computation, 2013, PRRB Publishing, ASIN B00D5E1S7W.

Architecture of Massively Parallel Microprocessor Systems, 2011, PRRB Publishing, ASIN B004K1F172.

Multicore Computer Architecture, 2014, PRRB Publishing, ASIN B00KB2XIQD.

Personal Robots, 2014, PRRB Publishing, ASIN B00MBQ084K.

RISC Microprocessors, History and Overview, 2013, PRRB Publishing, ASIN B00D5SCHQO.

Robots and Telerobots in Space Applications, 2011, PRRB Publishing, ASIN B0057IMJRM.

The Saturn Rocket and the Pegasus Missions, 1965, 2013, PRRB Publishing, ASIN B00BVA79ZW.

Microprocessors in Space, 2011, PRRB Publishing, ASIN B0057PFJQI.

Computer Virtualization and the Cloud, 2013, PRRB Publishing,

ASIN B00BAFF0JA.

What's the Worst That Could Happen? Bad Assumptions, Ignorance, Failures and Screw-ups in Engineering Projects, 2014, PRRB Publishing, ASIN B00J7SH540.

Computer Architecture & Programming of the Intel x86 Family, 2013, PRRB Publishing, ASIN B0078Q39D4.

The Hardware and Software Architecture of the Transputer, 2011, PRRB Publishing, ASIN B004OYTS1K.

Mainframes, Computing on Big Iron, 2015, PRRB Publishing, ASIN B00TXQQ3FI

Introduction to Spacecraft Control Centers, 2015, PRRB Publishing, 2016, ASIN B01D1Y5LZ0.

A Practitioner's Guide to RISC Microprocessor Architecture, Wiley-Interscience, 1996, ISBN 0471130184.

Embedded Computer Systems for Space, 2015, PRRB Publishing, ASIN B018BAYCCM.

Made in the USA
Lexington, KY
12 July 2017